The **33rd**
an anthology

DREXEL UNIVERSITY
College of
Arts and Sciences

DREXEL
PUBLISHING GROUP

Editor	Gail D. Rosen
Drexel Publishing Group Director	Scott Stein
Book Designer	Andrew Turner
Editorial Co-ops	Jack Davis
	Jahdae Gardener
Student Interns	Mahadhi Balaji
	Samir Bhalla
	Christopher Faunce
	Ciara Richards
	Šárka Richterova

Sponsors

Drexel University
The College of Arts and Sciences at Drexel University
The Department of English and Philosophy at Drexel University

Dr. Kelly Joyce, Interim Dean, College of Arts and Sciences, Drexel University
Dr. J. Roger Kurtz, Department Head, English and Philosophy, Drexel University

The 33rd Volume 14
Drexel University
Department of English and Philosophy
3141 Chestnut Street
Philadelphia, PA 19104
drexelpublishing.com

Cover photo by Kala F. Summers
Back Cover photo by Dylan Lam

Copyright © 2021 by the Drexel Publishing Group. All rights reserved.

The 33rd is published once a year.

Submissions are open in the spring, winter, and fall terms of each academic year. Manuscripts must be submitted as an e-mail attachment (MS Word). Visit drexelpublishing.com for submission guidelines.

ISBN 978-1-7324500-3-5

Deepest thanks to: Dr. Kelly Joyce; Dr. Norma Bouchard; Dr. J. Roger Kurtz; all the judges from the Drexel Publishing Group Creative Writing Contest (Stacey Ake, Jan Armon, Valerie Booth, Judy Curlee, Lisa DiMaio, Casey Hirsch, Henry Israeli, Greg Jewell, Lynn Levin, George MacMillan, Jill Moses, Karen Nulton, Margene Petersen, Sheila Sandapen, Doreen Saar, James Stieb, Kathleen Volk Miller); the Drexel Publishing Group Essay Contest (Stacey Ake, Ron Bishop, Anne Erickson, Jordan Hyatt, George MacMillan, Deirdre McMahon, Jonson Miller, Karen Nulton, Rakhmiel Peltz, Marilyn Piety, Don Riggs, Sheila Sandapen, Eric Schmutz, Fred Siegel, Errol Sull, Monica Togna); the First-Year Writing Contest (Jan Armon, Benjamin Barnett, Judy Curlee, Lisa DiMaio, Anne Erickson, Lea Jacobson, Liz Kimball, Rachel Kolman, Roger Kurtz, Deirdre McMahon, George MacMillan, Leah Mele, Chris Nielson, Karen Nulton, Margene Petersen, Gail D. Rosen, Sheila Sandapen, Fred Siegel, Scott Stein, Errol Sull, Maria Volynsky); the Department of English and Philosophy, especially Liz Heenan; contest participants; and the Drexel Publishing Group staff.

The fonts used within this publication are Laski Slab and Source Sans Pro.

XanEdu

Credits

Armon, Jan. "Rob—A Flash Memoir" was published in Alexandra Petri's online chat. "Petri Dishes," <live.washingtonpost.com>, on September 22, 2020.

Fox, Valerie. "Interpretation, For Bliss" appears in *Blink-Ink* (2021). "Our Komodo (A Kind of Love)" was published in *Cabinet of Heed 37* (2020).

Hyatt, Jordan. "Send First Vaccines to Pennsylvania's Prisons" was published on Dec 7, 2020, in *The Philadelphia Inquirer*.

Israeli, Henry. "To Have Lived Long Enough To Be Allowed To Return" was published in *Crab Creek Review* in February 2018.

Kaschock, Kirsten. "The Urgency of Being" was published in *Bennington Review*, Issue Eight, October 2020.

Kotzin, Miriam N. "Cairn" was published in *Doorknobs & Body Paint*, issue 36 (summer 2019). "Covid-19 2020" was published in *50-Word Stories*, Feb. 27, 2020. "I Tell My Therapist That My Mother's Lessons Didn't Hold Water" was published in *Blink-Ink* in June 2021. "That Takes the Cake" was published in *Doorknobs & Body Paint*, issue 34 (fall 2018).

Levin, Lynn. "Dr. Rieux, Meet Dr. Fauci: Seeing Albert Camus's *The Plague* with 2020 Vision" was published on *The Massachusetts Review* blog on October 22, 2020.

MacMillan, George A. "Fighting Solo: Covid-19 and the Single Parent" appeared in the anthology *After the Pandemic: Visions of Life Post COVID-19*, published by Sunbury Press, Mechanicsville, PA, on May 1, 2020.

Millan, Harriet Levin. "Green Fox Fur" was published in *Hamilton Stone Review*, Spring 2021.

Ottinger, Gwen. "Make Your Writing Workshops Effective" was published in *Write Now Philly*, January 22, 2020. https://writenowphilly.com/make-your-writing-workshops-effective.

Riggs, Don. "Review of Philip M. Cohen's *Nick Bones Underground*" was published in *The Future Fire Reviews* on February 25, 2021.

Sull, Errol Craig. "'Didja'—Word of the Year from COVID" was published in *The Buffalo News* on December 26th, 2020.

Warnock, Scott. "Let's Watch The News Together" was originally published July 30, 2020 on *When Falls the Coliseum*: http://whenfallsthecoliseum.com/2020/07/30lets-watch-the-news-together.

Welcome

At the 2021 College of Arts and Sciences commencement ceremony, University President John Fry called CoAS "the academic heart of Drexel." Year in and year out, *The 33rd* speaks to this truth.

This year's edition of the annual anthology is rich with the College's unique blend of interdisciplinary collaboration, field experience, and community engagement in the pursuit of knowledge, truth, and equity. CoAS students and faculty are a creative, engaged collection of scholars, teachers and learners, and a true credit to Drexel University.

Congratulations to the writers and editors of this edition of *The 33rd*. I hope you enjoy their work as much as I do.

Kelly Joyce, Ph.D.
Interim Dean, College of Arts and Sciences

Preface

Each year the Drexel Publishing Group collects and publishes outstanding writing by students and faculty from across our university to create this unique anthology that we call *The 33rd*. In your hands is our fourteenth volume.

All the essays and stories in this collection are adjudicated through a competitive review process. After publication, we use this volume as a textbook in many of our writing classes. The result is different every year, with new and creative surprises each time. What remains constant is the way that *The 33rd* embodies our mission of promoting imaginative and effective writing, starting right here on the street that gives the publication its name, and reaching out into a world that is limited only by our creative imagination.

We are especially proud that one of the entries in last year's edition of *The 33rd* was noticed and selected for re-publication in a major composition textbook from W.W. Norton. Renae Tingling's essay "Sleepless Nights of a University Student" will appear in the sixth edition of *The Norton Field Guide to Writing*. This is an impressive accomplishment for Renae, who wrote the essay in a first-year writing class with Professor Henry Israeli.

This is in fact the second year in a row that *The 33rd* has distinguished itself in this way. Sanjana Ramanathan's essay "An End to Sexism in Gaming Communities," from our 2019 volume, was selected for re-publication in the fifth edition of Norton's *They Say, I Say: The Moves that Matter in Academic Writing, with Readings*.

Cultivating curiosity and creativity in a supportive environment is the hallmark of the Department of English and Philosophy. Whether it's through our MFA in fiction writing, through our community-based learning courses that connect with organizations and institutions in greater Philadelphia, through our many internships, or through other initiatives from the Drexel Publishing Group like *The 33rd*, our students find multiple outlets for their writing to reach the world.

Enjoy!

J. Roger Kurtz, Ph.D.
Professor and Department Head
Department of English and Philosophy

Table of Contents
First-Year Writing

Nominees — 2
Introduction — 5

Winner
Lianna Wang — How Minority Disadvantages Lead to Disproportionate COVID-19 Rates — 7

First Runner-up
Elsa Panczner — The Facts of My Birth — 10

Second Runner-up
Abby Tabas — Social Media Activism: Changing the World from the Couch — 13

Honorable Mention
Jordan Anderson — Target — 16
Ana Fuciu — Give Credit Where Credit is Due—a Brief History of *Ia* — 19
Caroline Gallen — Take Nothing So That You Can Have Everything — 24
Sanjana Suresh — The Last Dance — 28
Marie Ann Tomaj — Why are Females so Often Misdiagnosed? — 32
Bethany White — Teach — 35
Cianni Williams — Corkscrew Curls — 37

Drexel Publishing Group Essays

Introduction — 43

Humanities

First Place
Gabrielle Werner — *Frankenstein,* Scientific Advancement, and the God Complex — 45

Second Place
Vivek Babu — The Television and The American Dream — 50

Honorable Mention
Arthi Sivendra — Democracy: America's Greatest Scam — 53

Social Sciences

First Place
Hope Wilson — Gender Roles and the Continued Imperialism of America — 56

Second Place
Sky Harper — Shidine'e doo Shidziil (My People, My Strength) — 59

Honorable Mention
Ellie DiPaolo — The Impact of Teacher Efficacy on Student Performance — 62
Samuel Weinstein — The Gravity of Personality — 65

The Zelda Provenzano Endowed STEM Writing Award

Vivek Babu	The Hygiene Hypothesis, Microbial "Old Friends," and the COVID-19 Pandemic	68
Emma Barnes	The Fast and the Fashionable: How Your Closet Contributes to a Global Crisis	74
María José Garcia	What About Us? Scientific, Technological, and Health Disparities	78

Drexel Publishing Group Creative Writing

Introduction 89

Creative Nonfiction

First Place
Max Gallagher — Cough Into My Open Mouth — 91

Second Place
Anh Quach — Tales from Quarantine — 93

Honorable Mention
Muntaha Haq — Things Unseen — 100

Fiction

First Place
Sanjana Ramanathan — The Lady of the Butterflies — 103

Second Place
Muntaha Haq — Green Melon Bars — 107

Honorable Mention
Mikayla Butz-Weidner — The Tragedy of Mr. and Mrs. Timothy Beckett — 110

Humor

First Place
Tim Hanlon — A Letter to Tony — 113

Second Place
Max Gallagher — Dog-Walking 101 — 116

Op-Ed

First Place
Nicky Como — Immigration's Effects on Children — 120

Poetry

First Place
Sanjana Ramanathan — Neon Odyssey — 122

Second Place
Sophie Geagan — intermission — 123

Honorable Mention
Sophie Geagan — Bloom — 124
Muntaha Haq — chocolate princess — 125

Writers Room

Introduction — 129

Dejah Jade	Hopeless Philly Boy	131
Alina Macneal	She Made It Look Easy	132
Kelly Bergh	Once, long, long ago	133
Eden Skye Einhorn	Late Night Reflections from a Weary Mind	134
Aaliyah Sesay	Easton	135

Faculty Writing

Introduction — 141

Jan Armon	Rob—A Flash Memoir	143
Valerie Fox	Interpretation, for Bliss	144
	Our Komodo (A Kind of Love)	145
Jordan Hyatt	Send First Vaccines to Pennsylvania's Prisons	147
Henry Israeli	To Have Lived Long Enough To Be Allowed To Return	149
Kirsten Kaschock	The Urgency of Being	150
Miriam N. Kotzin	Cairn	155
	Covid-19 2020	156
	I Tell My Therapist That My Mother's Lessons Didn't Hold Water	157
	That Takes the Cake	158
Lynn Levin	Dr. Rieux, Meet Dr. Fauci: Seeing Albert Camus's *The Plague* with 2020 Vision	159
George A. MacMillan	Fighting Solo: Covid-19 and the Single Parent	163
Harriet Levin Millan	Green Fox Fur	167
Gwen Ottinger	Make Your Writing Workshops Effective	170
Don Riggs	Review of Philip M. Cohen's *Nick Bones Underground*	172
Errol Craig Sull	"Didja"—Word of the Year from COVID	174
Scott Warnock	Let's Watch the News Together	176

Contributors — 181

Writings Arranged by Context

Argument

Vivek Babu	The Television and The American Dream	50
Emma Barnes	The Fast and the Fashionable: How Your Closet Contributes to a Global Crisis	74
Nicky Como	Immigration's Effects on Children	120
Ellie DiPaolo	The Impact of Teacher Efficacy on Student Performance	62
María José Garcia	What About Us?: Scientific, Technological, and Health Disparities	78
Jordan Hyatt	Send First Vaccines to Pennsylvania's Prisons	147
Arthi Sivendra	Democracy: America's Greatest Scam	53
Abby Tabas	Social Media Activism: Changing the World from the Couch	13
Marie Ann Tomaj	Why are Females so Often Misdiagnosed?	32
Lianna Wang	How Minority Disadvantages Lead to Disproportionate Covid-19 Rates	7
Samuel Weinstein	The Gravity of Personality	65
Hope Wilson	Gender Roles and the Continued Imperialism of America	56

Covid-19

Vivek Babu	The Hygiene Hypothesis, Microbial "Old Friends," and the COVID-19 Pandemic	68
María José Garcia	What About Us? Scientific, Technological, and Health Disparities	78
Tim Hanlon	A Letter to Tony	113
Jordan Hyatt	Send First Vaccines to Pennsylvania's Prisons	147
Miriam N. Kotzin	Covid-19 2020	156
Lynn Levin	Dr. Rieux, Meet Dr. Fauci: Seeing Albert Camus's *The Plague* with 2020 Vision	159
George A. MacMillan	Fighting Solo: Covid-19 and the Single Parent	163
Anh Quach	Tales from Quarantine	93
Errol Craig Sull	"Didja"—Word of the Year from COVID	174
Lianna Wang	How Minority Disadvantages Lead to Disproportionate Covid-19 Rates	7
Scott Warnock	Let's Watch the News Together	176

Education

Nicky Como	Immigration's Effects on Children	120
Ellie DiPaolo	The Impact of Teacher Efficacy on Student Performance	62
Lynn Levin	Dr. Rieux, Meet Dr. Fauci: Seeing Albert Camus's *The Plague* with 2020 Vision	159
Gwen Ottinger	Make Your Writing Workshops Effective	170
Samuel Weinstein	The Gravity of Personality	65
Bethany White	Teach	35

Ethics / Philosophy

Vivek Babu	The Hygiene Hypothesis, Microbial "Old Friends," and the COVID-19 Pandemic	68
Emma Barnes	The Fast and the Fashionable: How Your Closet Contributes to a Global Crisis	74
María José Garcia	What About Us?: Scientific, Technological, and Health Disparities	78
Arthi Sivendra	Democracy: America's Greatest Scam	53
Gabrielle Werner	*Frankenstein*, Scientific Advancement, and the God Complex	45
Hope Wilson	Gender Roles and the Continued Imperialism of America	56

Explanatory Writing

Vivek Babu	The Hygiene Hypothesis, Microbial "Old Friends," and the COVID-19 Pandemic	68
Vivek Babu	The Television and The American Dream	50
George A. MacMillan	Fighting Solo: Covid-19 and the Single Parent	163
Gwen Ottinger	Make Your Writing Workshops Effective	170
Arthi Sivendra	Democracy: America's Greatest Scam	53
Marie Ann Tomaj	Why are Females so Often Misdiagnosed?	32

Exploratory Writing

Nicky Como	Immigration's Effects on Children	120
Ellie DiPaolo	The Impact of Teacher Efficacy on Student Performance	62
Ana Fuciu	Give Credit Where Credit Is Due—A Brief History of *Ia*	19
Caroline Gallen	Take Nothing So That You Can Have Everything	24

Abby Tabas	Social Media Activism: Changing the World from the Couch	13
Samuel Weinstein	The Gravity of Personality	65
Gabrielle Werner	*Frankenstein*, Scientific Advancement, and the God Complex	45
Hope Wilson	Gender Roles and the Continued Imperialism of America	56

Fiction

Mikayla Butz-Weidner	The Tragedy of Mr. and Mrs. Timothy Beckett	110
Muntaha Haq	Green Melon Bars	107
Miriam N. Kotzin	Cairn	155
	Covid-19 2020	156
	I Tell My Therapist That My Mother's Lessons Didn't Hold Water	157
	That Takes the Cake	158
Sanjana Ramanathan	The Lady of the Butterflies	103

Gender, Race, and Culture

Jordan Anderson	Target	16
Ana Fuciu	Give Credit Where Credit is Due—a Brief History of *Ia*	19
Muntaha Haq	Green Melon Bars	107
	chocolate princess	125
	Things Unseen	100
Sky Harper	Shidine'e doo Shidziil (My People, My Strength)	59
Dejah Jade	Hopeless Philly Boy	131
Kirsten Kaschock	The Urgency of Being	150
Harriet Levin Millan	Green Fox Fur	167
Elsa Panczner	The Facts of My Birth	10
Anh Quach	Tales from Quarantine	93
Aaliyah Sesay	Easton	135
Sanjana Suresh	The Last Dance	28
Marie Ann Tomaj	Why are Females so Often Misdiagnosed?	32
Bethany White	Teach	35
Cianni Williams	Corkscrew Curls	37
Hope Wilson	Gender Roles and the Continued Imperialism of America	56

Humor

Jan Armon	Rob—A Flash Memoir	143
Max Gallagher	Dog-Walking 101	116
Tim Hanlon	A Letter to Tony	113
Errol Craig Sull	"Didja"—Word of the Year from COVID	174

Literary Criticism

Vivek Babu	The Television and The American Dream	50
Lynn Levin	Dr. Rieux, Meet Dr. Fauci: Seeing Albert Camus's *The Plague* with 2020 Vision	159
Don Riggs	Review of Philip M. Cohen's *Nick Bones Underground*	172
Gabrielle Werner	*Frankenstein*, Scientific Advancement, and the God Complex	45

Memoir / Personal Narrative

Jordan Anderson	Target	16
Jan Armon	Rob—A Flash Memoir	143
Max Gallagher	Cough Into My Open Mouth	91
	Dog-Walking 101	116
Muntaha Haq	Things Unseen	100
Sky Harper	Shidine'e doo Shidziil (My People, My Strength)	59
Kirsten Kaschock	The Urgency of Being	150
Alina Macneal	She Made It Look Easy	132
Gwen Ottinger	Make Your Writing Workshops Effective	170
Elsa Panczner	The Facts of My Birth	10
Anh Quach	Tales from Quarantine	93
Aaliyah Sesay	Easton	135
Errol Craig Sull	"Didja"—Word of the Year from COVID	174
Sanjana Suresh	The Last Dance	28
Bethany White	Teach	35
Cianni Williams	Corkscrew Curls	37

Poetry

Kelly Bergh	Once, long, long ago	133
Eden Skye Einhorn	Late Night Reflections from a Weary Mind	134
Valerie Fox	Interpretation, for Bliss	144
Valerie Fox	Our Komodo (A Kind of Love)	145

Sophie Geagan	intermission	123
Sophie Geagan	Bloom	124
Muntaha Haq	chocolate princess	125
Henry Israeli	To Have Lived Long Enough To Be Allowed To Return	149
Dejah Jade	Hopeless Philly Boy	131
Alina Macneal	She Made It Look Easy	132
Harriet Levin Millan	Green Fox Fur	167
Sanjana Ramanathan	Neon Odyssey	122

Politics

Emma Barnes	The Fast and the Fashionable: How Your Closet Contributes to a Global Crisis	74
María José Garcia	What About Us?: Scientific, Technological, and Health Disparities	78
Tim Hanlon	A Letter to Tony	113
Jordan Hyatt	Send First Vaccines to Pennsylvania's Prisons	147
Arthi Sivendra	Democracy: America's Greatest Scam	53
Abby Tabas	Social Media Activism: Changing the World from the Couch	13
Scott Warnock	Let's Watch the News Together	176
Hope Wilson	Gender Roles and the Continued Imperialism of America	56

Profile

Ana Fuciu	Give Credit Where Credit Is Due—A Brief History of *Ia*	19
Caroline Gallen	Take Nothing So That You Can Have Everything	24

Science

Vivek Babu	The Hygiene Hypothesis, Microbial "Old Friends," and the COVID-19 Pandemic	68
Emma Barnes	The Fast and the Fashionable: How Your Closet Contributes to a Global Crisis	74
María José Garcia	What About Us?: Scientific, Technological, and Health Disparities	78

First-Year Writing

First-Year Writing Nominees

The following students were nominated for the First-Year Writing Contest.
Congratulations to all!

Rawad Albarouki
Munazzah Al Hashim
Renee Amos
Tarana Ananna
Eric Andreski
Amira Aspromonte
Pauline Autard
Aishwarya Bahl
Henry Bailey
Cole Bardin
Serenity Baruzzini
Gracie Bertsche
Marta Brennan
Ann Bui
Sofia Caballero
Olivia Callender
Waverli Chu
Lauren Corcoran
Erin Cornella
Amanda Cummings
Emily Daly
Elizabeth Davidar
Gillian Dengler
Hillary Devlen
Lia DiMitri
Thien Doan
Sally Ehlers
Mark El Moujabber
Corinne Farley
Grace Fisher
Adam Goldstein
Emara Gordon
Gabrielle Greco
Isobel Grudin
Joseph Gruzinski
Muntaha Haq
Emily McKinley Hill
Anh Ho
Sarah Hong
Di Huynh
Lydia Janik
Gisele Kahlon
Parker Keskinen
Anastasia Kolker
Ethan Kraycik
Zoe Kronish
Megan Kyte
Kaylin Laghaei
Sebastien Lebron
Gabriella Lewald
Ivy Li
Joyce Li
Jenny Lin
Judy Luong

Aaron Marks
Therese Martin
Rachel Danielle Miller
Reeghan Miller
Griffin Mitchell
Jacob Moore
Ruth Nawy
Dat Tuan Nguyen
Dune Nguyen
Josephine Nguyen
Xuan Nguyen
Cailean O'Brien
Colin Page
Kenneth Pagliei
Mary Pham
Matic Pham
Alesha Philip
Ethan Quigley
Kaylee Rodriguez
Julianna Rogers
Srija Saha
Sotonye Sam-Epelle
David Saunders
Angelina Scavitto
Camryn Schroder
Joanna Scorese
Mitchell Shapiro

Christopher Sherman
Jake Simms
Ella Simring
Aryaman Singha
Sukethram Sivakumar
Alicia So
Jeanna Stedman
Griffin Stein
Hannah Stern
Maggie Stillman
Will Soleo
Nishan Thapa
Morgan Tiziker
Kimberly Toich
Matthew Traynor
Giorgio Vadarlis
Thomas Vaughan
Kriti Verma
Anastasia Voldeidze
David Weems
Michael Wertz
Kesia Zachariah
Steven Zafiris-Gerohimos
Adil Zeinullayev
John Zheng
Adel Zhumanova

Introduction

As the Director of the First-Year Writing Program, I work with over 60 dedicated instructors who coach, cajole, and mentor 2,500-3,000 incoming students who produce tens of thousands of pages of writing. One of the best parts of my job is working with Jill Moses, our Assistant Director, on the First-Year Writing Contest.

This section of *The 33rd* includes essays written by the winners, runners-up, and honorable mentions from the contest that ran in the 2020-2021 academic year. Here is how the essays get from the classroom into this book:

- Students work very hard in their classes to produce lively, engaging writing about themselves and the world around them. Their instructors work hard, too, giving advice and encouragement throughout the writing process.

- Towards the end of the fall, we ask instructors to invite no more than two students from each of their sections to submit their best work to the First-Year Writing Contest. Last year, we got 115 excellent entries.

- With the help of approximately 20 faculty members, we go through a two-step judging process. After much deliberation, the judges come up with a winner, a first runner-up, a second runner-up, and seven honorable mentions.

- During the spring term, the winners, runners-up, and honorable mentions are announced at the English Awards Ceremony, along with the winners of various other contests. Furthermore, our winners receive prizes supported by a very generous endowment from the Erika Guenther and Gertrud Daemmrich Memorial Prizes.

- Finally, the editors of *The 33rd* step in to get permissions, to edit, and to create the book you are holding.

So, here is *The 33rd*. Your instructors in the First-Year Writing Program will ask you to read essays that won prizes last year so you can discuss them, debate them, and learn from them.

Are you interested in writing? Will you be in this book next year? On behalf of the First-Year Writing Program, we look forward to reading your work.

Fred Siegel, Ph.D.
Director of the First-Year Writing Program

Winner—First-Year Writing

Evaluating and Solving Problems: For this assignment, you will research a problematic issue, propose one or more solutions to the problem, and present an argument supporting your solution. One effective way to approach this assignment is to identify a problem in a profession or discipline of interest to you. Another is to deal with a problem local to Drexel, Philadelphia, or your hometown, and relevant to your experience there. The topic should be original and significant.

—Professor Robert Finegan

Lianna Wang

How Minority Disadvantages Lead to Disproportionate COVID-19 Rates

On March 21, 2020, Jason Hargrove, a Black bus driver in Detroit, had a woman cough on his bus multiple times without covering her mouth. When he got home, Hargrove uploaded a passionate video rant onto Facebook to express his frustrations about her actions, especially amid a pandemic. In the video, he explains that he "can't stay home, we out here as public workers trying to do our job, trying to make an honest living, trying to care of our families." Four days later, Hargrove began to feel sick, and within a week, he died of the virus (Harrison).

For many racial minorities such as Black, Indigenous, and Latinx people, this type of story is unfortunately familiar. According to an August 2029 CDC study, in comparison to white people, African Americans are at a 2.6 times higher risk of catching coronavirus, while American Indians and Latino people are at a 2.8 times higher risk ("COVID-19 Hospitalization"). To put those numbers in perspective, the APM Research Lab, whose staff has been tracking COVID-19 deaths by race from April to September, stated that "if they had died of COVID-19 at the same actual rate as White Americans, about 20,800 Black, 10,900 Latino, 700 Indigenous, and 80 Pacific Islander Americans would still be alive" (APM Research Lab). Even President Trump recognized the severity of COVID's impact on the minority communities, asking in a coronavirus press briefing on April 7th, "But why is it that the African American community is so much, you know, numerous times more than everybody else? [sic]" (United States, James S. Brady Press Briefing Room).

The answer to his question lies within the deep-rooted educational and economic disparity between minorities and white people that has been plaguing America for decades. Because many minority communities do not have access to high-quality education in their low-income areas, Black, Indigenous, and Latinx youth are less likely to finish high school or pursue college than their white and Asian American peers. According to the government-run National Center for Education Statistics, "The U.S. average ACGR (Adjusted Cohort Graduation Rate) of White public high school students was 10 percentage points higher than the U.S. average ACGR for their Black peers in 2017–18"

(NCES). With lower rates of high school completion and college entrances, minority youths are less likely to secure stable, high paying jobs. Consequently, the lack of educational support and resources available to ethnic minorities because of their economic circumstances creates an opportunity gap between them and non-minorities of color.

This opportunity gap is a problem within itself, but the severity of the problem grows in the context of the current COVID-19 pandemic. The less secure, lower-paying jobs that the opportunity gap forces minorities of color to work are oftentimes in workplaces and fields such as transportation, healthcare facilities, grocery stores, and factories. These are considered essential jobs and push people of color to the frontlines where they are at higher exposure to the virus ("Health Equity"). Unfortunately, due to limited job options resulting from their lack of education, many ethnic minorities cannot afford to leave these jobs, even if it puts them at risk of contracting the virus. Additionally, low-income ethnic minorities find themselves living in overcrowded situations such as low-income and public housing, especially during the current pandemic when unemployment rates have caused eviction and homelessness to skyrocket. Overcrowding poses a huge problem amidst the global pandemic because living in crowded communities that make it difficult to social distance or self-isolate expedites the spread of the virus ("Health Equity"). People can argue that by the same logic, white people with low incomes are also affected heavily, so the problem is not related to race. While this is true, aside from Asians, minorities of color are generally more likely to have lower incomes. According to Duke University sociology professor Linda M. Burton, "in the most recent data from 2015, one in four blacks and Native Americans, and one in five Hispanics are poor," contrasting with "one in ten Whites and Asians" (Burton). For these reasons, communities of color are at a higher risk of exposure to the virus, which is why minority rates of COVID-19 are so much higher than those of non-minorities.

Luckily, solutions are available. The CDC says that the best way "to prevent the spread of COVID-19" is to "work together to ensure that people have resources to maintain and manage their physical and mental health, including easy access to information, affordable testing, and medical and mental health care" ("Health Equity"). Thus, one short-term immediate solution is making coronavirus testing fast, affordable, and especially accessible to communities of color. In a case study investigating the availability of testing in relation to income and race, NPR reported that "in four out of six of the largest cities in Texas, testing sites are disproportionately located in whiter neighborhoods" (McMinn). If more testing sites were situated in communities of color, minorities could get tested faster and as a result, get treated faster. The faster someone gets diagnosed, the faster they can self-isolate and stop the spread.

While short term solutions like accessible testing can offer immediate relief, a more long-term solution would be to decrease the education gap between racial minorities and non-minorities, which could be done by increasing funding for education in low-income areas with people of color. With more funding, students will have access to higher quality education and resources to further their knowledge. In his book, *Closing the Education Gap:*

Benefits and Costs, Peter Rydell explains that "an additional external benefit of education is its effect on the use of government programs, most particularly the means-tested programs such as welfare, food stamps, Medicaid, and other social redistributive programs" (Rydell). By applying these short-term and long-term solutions, the growing educational and economic disparity between communities of color and non-minority communities can be minimized, providing economic stability and better resources so that minorities will be less affected in health crises.

Works Cited

APM Research Lab Staff. (2020). "COVID-19 Deaths Analyzed by Race and Ethnicity." Retrieved October 07, 2020, from https://www.apmresearchlab.org/covid/deaths-by-race.

Burton, Linda M. "The Stanford Center on Poverty and Inequality."*The Poverty and InequalityReport, Race and Ethnicity.* CDC. (2020, August 18). "COVID-19 Hospitalization and Death by Race/Ethnicity." RetrievedOctober 07, 2020, from https://www.cdc.gov/coronavirus/2019-ncov/covid-data/investigations-discovery/hospitalization-death-by-race-ethnicity.html.

CDC. (2020). "Health Equity Considerations and Racial and Ethnic Minority Groups." Retrieved October 07, 2020, from https://www.cdc.gov/coronavirus/2019-ncov/community/health-equity/race-ethnicity.html.

Harrison, Cameron. "Widow Begs Public to Stay Home during Coronavirus after Husband's Death."*ABC News*, ABC News Network, 6 Apr. 2020, abcnews.go.com/GMA/News/widow-begs-public-stay-home-coronavirus-husbands-death/story?id=69995034.

McMinn, Sean, et al. "In Large Texas Cities, Access To Coronavirus Testing May Depend On Where You Live." *NPR*, 27 May 2020,www.npr.org/sections/health-shots/2020/05/27/862215848/across-texas-black-and-hispanic-neighborhoods-have-fewer-coronavirus-testing-sites.

Rydell, C. Peter, et al. *Closing the Education Gap:Benefits and Costs*, RAND Corporation, 1999. ProQuest Ebook Central, https://ebookcentral-proquest-com. ezproxy2.library.drexel.edu/lib/drexel-ebooks/detail.action?docID=3031518.

United States, James S. Brady Press Briefing Room. "Remarks by President Trump, Vice President Pence, and Members of the Coronavirus Task Force in Press Briefing." The White House, 7 April 2020, https://www.whitehouse.gov/briefings-statements/remarks-president-trump-vice-president-pence-members-coronavirus-task-force-press-briefing-april-7-2020.

First Runner-up—First-Year Writing

Write about something so important to you that you feel compelled to write about it.

—Dr. Jan Armon

Elsa Panczner
The Facts of My Birth

Nineteen years ago, I was abandoned by my birth parents in Guilin, China. Fifteen months later, a white American couple adopted me. That is everything I know about my origin and it's what I spent my childhood building my identity on.

Sometimes I wish I could tell my younger self some special words that would make my childhood easier. The older I grew, the more I understood that identity is not a static version of myself at any given point in time, but a forever changing and developing concept that is shaped by how I interact with the world. However, even with this understanding, it is incredibly hard for me to come to terms with a part of my identity that was decided for me—being an Asian-American adoptee. I've never been able to feel quite Asian or entirely American and constantly struggle to find my place somewhere in-between. Perhaps laying out my experiences throughout my life can help decipher this 19-year-old code.

Section I: Culture Out of My Control

Before adopting me and my sister, my mother and father were required to attend adoption seminars. The psychologists who hosted these seminars made it very clear that when adopting internationally, new parents must keep their child connected to the child's birth heritage in order to foster psychological growth. In my pre-adolescence, I went to "Chinese School" on Saturday mornings for eight years, where the majority of other students were Chinese kids and Chinese parents who were practicing their native language. I went on visits to Chinatown in Philadelphia and my parents bought me lion dance costumes, colorful umbrellas, and wooden fans to wield. In elementary school, around the Lunar (Chinese) New Year, my parents would send me to school with fortune cookies and all my China Town goodies to teach my classmates about my culture.

My parents surrounded me with Chinese culture so that I could feel "connected to people who look like [me], who could teach [me] the culture that [they] could not." I can't imagine the pressure that parents of international adoptees face when it comes to preserving their child's heritage—but it was clear to me, at a very young age, that I didn't belong to Chinese culture. My first memories take place in Glen Mills, Pennsylvania. My parents are white Americans, my neighbors are white Americans, and I am American.

Section II: "Chinese"

Growing up, it didn't take long for me to realize that people who are not clearly white Americans will frequently be questioned about their ethnicity. Unfortunately, many times my answer of "American" or even "Asian-American" did not satisfy people's curiosities. Why must I elaborate on the ethnicity *I* have chosen to identify with? I very quickly grew to resent labeling myself as "Chinese."

I think the word "Chinese" began to be uncomfortable for me when I left the innocence of elementary school teasing and entered the sixth grade. I had two Chinese friends in elementary school: Emily, who was also a Chinese-American adoptee and my "BFFL" (best friend for life), and Caitlyn, whose Chinese parents immigrated to America shortly after having her. When I started middle school, not only did I experience all the perks of becoming an adolescent, but I w[as sep]arated from Emily and Caitlyn. The population at my middle school [was similar to] my elementary school, but the ratio of white students to [others bec]ame. This is about the time when the narrow[...] was incredibly uncomfortable f[...] never directed at me. [...] ounds and pulling bac[...] heless, seeing and hea[...] not that it offended me [...] at to me for the purpo[...]

Section III: [...]

In the [...] lost that I suppressed [...] much that I actually e[...] ally realized fitting in [...] narily white communi[...] From a group of friend[...] Asian Squad" was for [...] n immigrants and a few [...] ves the "Asian Squad" and freely expre[...]. We have since all gone our separate ways, but for a ye[...] eing Asian.

Section IV: (Actually) Growing Up

Between sections I and III, I've typed "Chinese" twelve times. I can now say I am sick of the word again. When used in relation to myself, the word makes my skin crawl.

Throughout high school and my year-long journey through adulthood, I've since become more comfortable with expressing my identity. In my high school, everyone was far too concerned about their own lives to bother me about mine. At times, I'll admit, I kind of forget I look Asian and go about my life as if I were any regular white American. As of now, it's just times where I hear slurs, stereotypes, and politically charged comments that bring back the pain. I now embrace my identity as an Asian-American adoptee in a way that also expresses who I am, regardless of the circumstances of my birth. Besides my appearance, I live the life of a regular 21st century white American student. As a part of my self-formed identity, I do intend to get a tattoo that will be one of my only ties to the culture of my birthplace—in Chinese characters: "Mother, Father, Connected Heart."

Section V: The Present (this very moment of writing)

I read sections I through IV to my boyfriend, Kyle, whose house I am currently sitting in. It took me a moment of staring and fidgeting until I was ready to read. "I feel incredibly awkward reading this aloud and am horrified thinking other people will read this," I told him. He took my hands and told me it was okay, and I began to read. Following my reading, Kyle released my hands, thanked me for sharing this, and embraced me. "I never see you any different than me," he said. "You are just as American as I am."

My reason for writing this piece was to figure out where I stand between the labeled boundaries of being Asian and American. I don't think I will ever be able to answer that question, as the world is constantly changing and so am I. Perhaps when I have children, I will have to face this dilemma all over again. However, I think I can follow up on my thought of what I could tell my younger self that would make my journey as an Asian-American adoptee easier: "You are more than the facts of your birth."

Second Runner-up—First-Year Writing

Evaluating and Solving Problems: For this assignment, you will research a problematic issue, propose one or more solutions to the problem, and present an argument supporting your solution. One effective way to approach this assignment is to identify a problem in a profession or discipline of interest to you. Another is to deal with a problem local to Drexel, Philadelphia, or your hometown, and relevant to your experience there. The topic should be original and significant.

—Professor Robert Finegan

Abby Tabas
Social Media Activism: Changing the World from the Couch

On June second, allies of the Black Lives Matter movement decided to show support by participating in a Blackout Tuesday event. Thousands of people posted black squares to their social media to raise awareness for the horrific treatment of Black Americans by police. While this simple act might seem like a good way to raise awareness for an important movement, there were some unforeseen issues. By including common tags associated with the Black Lives Matter movement on these black square posts, supporters were essentially clogging these channels with thousands of empty pictures, which disrupted the flow of important updates and information vital for those protesting in person. When people searched tags associated with the movement, the results were filled with rows of black squares, instead of the real-time information many rely on. According to a CNN article about the situation, "[v]isibility for different groups and activist projects are key right now," with many people staying updated by "monitoring or searching tags" (Willingham). This attempt to aid the movement perfectly represents the shortcomings of digital activism. Because posting a black square to Instagram or Twitter seems like an easy way to show support, many people were likely to participate without thinking of the effects it would have on the larger Black Lives Matter social media presence. The failure of this Blackout Tuesday event is indicative of larger problems with online activism, which include the disconnect between online and in-person activism.

This disconnect is explored by Ph.D. candidate at UNC Charlotte, Alireza Karduni. His study focuses on analyzing how the response to police shooting Keith Lamont Scott in Charlotte, North Carolina took place. The study concluded that the role of social media existed in two different groups, "one group involved with social media, local community and urban space." The second participated "exclusively through social media." This disconnect was mirrored when analyzing popular tweets focusing on the protests, where the study found that none of the top 20 tweets criticizing the protests were local to Charlotte, and those tweeting in support of the protests were split between local and non-local (Karduni). The significant amount of protest supporters who engaged only through social media point to a disconnect between those supporting a movement exclusively online, and those who are participating in person. This type of disconnect is what led to the failed Blackout Tuesday event, because those participating exclusively through social media were unable to consider the consequences of their activism on the spread of real-time, local information.

Another aspect of this disconnect comes in the form of performative activism, which refers to the practice of engaging in surface level activism online to gain praise. A recent example of this is the controversy over the French film *Cuties* which Netflix promoted in August. The film follows the journey of Senegalese Muslim girl, Amy, as she struggles to balance her desire to rebel against her conservative upbringing and the oversexualization of teenage girls in society. According to Salamishah Tillet from *The New York Times*, "Netflix... releas[ed] an ill-advised publicity image of tween girls puckering their lips for the camera. In response, the hashtag #CancelNetflix went viral." The massive criticism of this film on social media led to calls for the Department of Justice to open a child pornography investigation on Netflix (Tillet). The surface-level criticisms of *Cuties* on social media portray a film grappling with and condemning the sexualization of teen girls as an act of oversexualization itself, which completely ignores the main message of the narrative. The performative nature of these mass-criticisms is additionally exposed when we consider that the backlash is silencing the film's director, Maïmouna Doucouré, who drew on personal experience when developing *Cuties*. The backlash *Cuties* has received exemplifies how activism that relies on surface-level understanding and low-effort actions can harm the cause it appears to be championing.

In addition to harming the movements it takes place in, low effort activism leaves people vulnerable to misinformation. According to Keonyoung Park, a doctoral student researching social media activism at Syracuse University, organizations can promote types of low-effort, or instant activism, like sharing a post, in people with low levels of prior knowledge. This creates temporary, disingenuous support surrounding a movement. One of her studies, which focused on the degree to which people interacted with hoax information surrounding GMOs on Facebook, found that the "targeted individuals in instant activism are conceptualized as members of the instant public, who... participate in social media activism without serious consideration." The study also concluded that people who were more involved with GMO labeling outside of Facebook were less likely to believe hoax information. This indicates that types of online activism promoting simple, quick engagement rather than promoting independent research or long-term action can lead people to be more accepting of false information. With the already rampant amount of misinformation present online regarding serious issues, like Covid-19 and the upcoming election, we cannot afford to let instant activism instill more susceptibility to misinformation.

To make the most of social media activism, the way existing platforms handle content about political and social activism needs to shift away from prioritizing maximum user engagement. Currently, social media platforms are designed to engage users as much as possible, for as long as possible. According to former technology engineer, Aza Raskin, "designers were driven to create addictive app features by the business models of... [social media] companies"

(Andersson). Features like infinite scrolling "allow users to endlessly swipe… content without clicking" (Andersson). This design discourages users from leaving the app, which makes actions like fact checking or independently researching posts less likely. To encourage informed interaction, social media companies could create separate sections of existing platforms specifically for real-time, informal news, political movements, and social activism. These sections would not employ the current, addicting aspects of social media design. This would allow activists to take advantage of the large audience and widespread communication capabilities of current platforms, without encouraging the low-effort engagement that leads to issues seen within instant activism today.

Works Cited

Andersson, Hilary. "Social Media Apps Are 'Deliberately' Addictive to Users." *BBC News*, BBC, 3 July 2018, www.bbc.com/news/technology-44640959.

Karduni, Alireza, and Eric Sauda. "Anatomy of a Protest: Spatial Information, Social Media, and Urban Space." *Social Media + Society*, Jan. 2020, doi:10.1177/2056305119897320.

Park, Keonyoung, and Hyejoon Rim. "'Click First!': The Effects of Instant Activism Via a Hoax on Social Media." *Social Media + Society*, Apr. 2020, doi:10.1177/2056305120904706.

Tillet, Salamishah. "What the 'Cuties' Critics Can't See: The Complexities of Black Girlhood." *The New York Times*, 2 Oct. 2020, www.nytimes.com/2020/10/02/movies/cuties-netflix.html.

Willingham, AJ. "Why Posting a Black Image with the 'Black Lives Matter' Hashtag Could Be Doing More Harm than Good." *CNN*, Cable News Network, 2 June 2020, www.cnn.com/2020/06/02/us/blackout-tuesday-black-lives-matter-instagram-trnd/index.html.

Honorable Mention—First-Year Writing

Write about something so important to you that you feel compelled to write about it.

—Dr. Jan Armon

Jordan Anderson
Target

> "Black boys became criminalized. I was in constant dread for their lives, because they were targets everywhere. They still are."—Toni Morrison, 1998

My brother woke up that chilly February morning like he did every morning for school. His alarm, set for 6:30, went off with a loud "beep," initiating the start of his day. Hearing this raucous sound, his eyes fluttered open, and an exasperated groan left his throat. After tiredly pressing the snooze button in a huff, he rolled back over, anxious to get a few more moments of precious sleep. Fifteen minutes later, he knew he must get up. He staggered to the bathroom, quickly brushed his teeth, washed his face, and brushed his hair. Looking at the time, he realized he needed to hurry or risk missing his bus. He hurriedly threw on his clothes and flew down the stairs. As usual, there was no time to make a proper breakfast. Instead, he grabbed an apple from off the counter, swung his backpack over his shoulder, and made his way to the bus stop. As he got to the edge of the pavement, the bus slowly turned onto the street. He dashed across the street, and just as he reached the bus stop, the bus pulled up. One by one, the kids ahead of him filed onto the bus that would take them to middle school and took their seats. As my brother got on the bus and slumped down into his usual seat, he had not realized that there was a target on his back.

The school day was typical. His first two classes were rough, and he struggled to keep his eyes open. By the third class, he was able to focus, and he was eager to get through it. Lunch was next, and he was looking forward to eating a meal and hanging out with his friends. As soon as the lunch bell rang, he speed-walked with the sea of kids to the cafeteria and immediately got in the line to get a sandwich. He got his sandwich toasted as always, and after paying for it, he sat down at his usual table with his friends. The lunch period seemed to fly by, and as the bell rang, the students ambled to their first afternoon class. His afternoon classes went by without a hitch, and before he knew it, there were only fifteen minutes left of school. His eyes glued to the clock; he watched the seconds tick down. Soon there were ten minutes left, then five, and as he watched the clock strike three, the bell rang. Like a dam breaking open, kids flooded out of their classrooms and into the hallways, and he made his way to the bus. As he got to the bus circle and boarded the bus, a wave of calmness set over him. His day was finally over, and he was so close to being back to the place he felt the most secure: home.

The bright afternoon sun gleamed through the bus window and forced his eyes to flutter open. He had fallen asleep and thankfully had woken up in time. The bus was just turning down his street and would be at his stop in a few seconds. Preparing to disembark, he gathered his things and slung his backpack on his shoulder. As the bus slowed to a stop, he stood up and followed other kids off the bus. As his feet left the bus stairs and hit the pavement, all he could think about was taking a much-needed nap and relaxing. All he needed to do was cross the street. He looked both ways, but then, he paused. There was a cop car parked just a few feet down from the house. This was peculiar because he had never seen a police car on this street before. Not thinking much of it, he crossed the street and began to walk up the driveway. As he stepped onto the porch, key in hand, he heard the nearby sound of a car engine. He turned toward the sound and saw the same police car that was on the street, driving into the driveway. An immediate pang of confusion entered his body. *What could the police want? Was there some kind of trouble, or situation?* The possibility that he could be the reason had not crossed his mind.

He watched the police car come to a stop and the engine switch off, and then out stepped an officer. He was white, about six feet, two inches tall, and well-built. As the officer walked towards him, my brother's heart sank and fear filled the pit of his stomach. Now, he was scared.

"What are you doing here?" the officer asked, staring into his eyes.

In a jumble of a frenzy of words, he answered that he was going into his house and that he had just come home from school.

"Do you have an ID?" the officer coldly replied.

My brother uneasily responded that he had a school ID, but he thinks it is in his room. The officer then told him to go get it. My brother immediately fumbled through his keys, until he landed on the one for the front door. With the officer's eyes peering over his shoulder, he shakily unlocked the door. Grasping the door handle he swung it open just enough for him to get through, but the officer pulled the door open wider and unlawfully entered the house. Too preoccupied to think about the fact that the officer had entered the house without permission, he ran upstairs to his room. Trashing his room, he looked anywhere he could imagine his ID to be. After about five minutes of no luck, he began to get worried. *What would happen if he couldn't find his ID?* He then thought that maybe the ID was in his backpack. Running back down the stairs, he found his backpack in the place he left it, in the doorway, and next to it stood the officer. Heart beating out of his chest, he ripped his backpack open and dumped out the contents. He always kept a messy backpack, but somehow found the ID through the mess of paper and school supplies on the floor. Thankful he had found it, he politely handed it to the officer. The officer took the ID and examined it for what felt like hours. After the officer was satisfied, he began interrogating my brother.

"Do you live here? What were you doing here? Where are you coming from?"

The questions never seemed to end, but he made sure to answer them in the most polite way he could. He was aware of what could happen if an officer felt disrespected. After about ten minutes of questioning, the officer simply said, "Have a nice day," and left.

Immediately after he left, my brother called my mom and told her what had occurred. She contacted the police department and asked to speak to the officer that came to the house. The officer was dispatched back to the house, and he spoke to my mom in the very same spot he had just interrogated her son in. As my mother questioned the officer, he averted his eyes, rarely matching her glance. The reason he gave for questioning my brother was that there had been recent break-ins in the area with people wearing red shirts. As the officer finished his explanation, he spoke one last chilling statement:

"Your son was very respectful, ma'am."

The officer left our house for the second time that day, and just like that, it was over. For the officer at least. He continued with his day, went home to his family, probably not feeling like that day was any different than the rest. But for my brother and my family that day was special. It was special because even though my brother will always have a memory of the experience, he will be okay. My family and I were, of course, angry at the officer for abusing his power, but my only emotion now is thankfulness. Unlike many other black boys, my brother lived.

Honorable Mention—First-Year Writing

Use primary and secondary research to write a profile about a specific topic, such as a favorite food, artist, or art object. Explore the nature of your topic and why it matters. Although you may include memories to establish personal connections to the topic, the meat of this essay is what you discover by researching and writing about your topic.

—Professor Maegan Poland

Ana Fuciu

Give Credit Where Credit is Due—a Brief History of *Ia*

I received my first *ia* when I was just beginning to have a sense of my own life on earth. I believe it was the anniversary of my second lap around the sun when I first got acquainted with it (see photo of me with my grandparents on my 2nd birthday, 2004). Back then, I was not aware of the significance of this gift in my culture; all I knew is that I felt like a little princess who got a new ball gown and couldn't stop showing it off. You might have no idea what this thing is that I am talking about. First things first, *ia* is the name for the Romanian women's blouse. It comes from the Latin "tunicae linea" which translates to a straight, thin linen tunic (Gheorghiță).

The blouse has a history that dates back centuries—and I dare say even millennia. It is more than just a folk costume item used by women to cover themselves; it is a symbol of femininity, grace and uniqueness. Each *ia* is unique. The traditional way of weaving it includes a wooden loom, along with a very patient and passionate seamstress. It has all sorts of embroidery, motifs and seams that are carefully sewn on the clothing piece after weaving. The motifs differ from one region to the other, as well as the color scheme and sometimes even the material it is confected from; *ia* can be made from cotton, homemade mulberry silk, linen, or hemp. Serving a great range of purposes, from being a day-to-day item to wedding attire, *ia* has both an individual and collective significance for each Romanian woman who wears it.

My grandma is the one who introduced the importance of conserving our ancestral heritage to me. She has three boys—my dad and his two brothers—so she has never experienced the joy of dressing up a toddler girl. I suspect she even prepared this attire for my 2nd birthday long before I was born, hoping that I would turn out to be a girl. I called my grandma to find out more about her relationship with *ia*.

"How did I react when you dressed me up on my birthday?" I asked.

She laughed.

"How do you think?! You were glowing as you always do," she said. "You had no idea what that costume was, but it didn't matter. Maybe your sixth sense felt its value."

"When did you receive your first one?" I asked.

"Oh Lord, it must've been in elementary school. Back [in the 1950s] you couldn't find anything to wear here."

The Communist regime had just settled in 1947; in the 1950s, peasants were left without their lands which became state owned. They had to find means to dress their children for school—so women were forced to carry on the tradition for the sake of their families.

"Mamma weaved me blouses for school that I wore until I grew out of them. But the first embroidered one... in middle school when we started having school feasts," she said.

"Mamma? Did she know how to weave?"

"Yes, she learnt it from her mother. And her mother from her grandmother. Those were the only passions peasant women had. Weaving and sewing."

I never knew this about my great-grandma. Last year, my grandma gifted to me another *ia*, very different from the ones I already had. I never got to ask her about the blouse's origin.

"So, is the blue one you gave me last Christmas woven by Mamma?"

"Yes, she made it for me when I was 18 to wear it at the [traditional Transylvanian Christmas] dance. That's where your grandpa courted me."

After turning 18, girls were due to marry as soon as possible. Around Christmas time, there were a lot of traditions and customs happening in rural areas, including this type of dance event. Only unmarried girls were allowed to participate, and it was widely known that single boys made them advances for the purpose of marriage. Also, it was a time to show off their newly-woven garments.

"Wow, I had no idea. Did women wear them at work also besides feast days?"

"Of course they did. Before we found clothes in stores, Mamma wove at the loom blouses for every season and occasion. Woollen for winter, sheer linen for summer in the fields. They weren't only holy day attire" (M.Fuciu).

After talking to her, I realized once again why I felt so connected to my heritage. I mean, how can I not when I descend from so many generations of skilled women? It's already in my DNA.

Folklore has developed throughout the tumultuous history of humanity in communities where literacy was mostly non-existent. As Roxana Claudia

Tompea states in her article "The #GiveCredit Campaign and Why It Matters: A Case Study of La blouse Roumaine," illiterate peasants who relied on orality expressed themselves through signs and symbols placed on pottery, decorations, and clothing which depicted their narratives, sufferings, and creeds. This is how folklore fashion came to life. After meeting the basic need of warmth and protection, folk costumes serve the role of a history book to us. They are proof that our ancestors' existence goes far beyond the earthly and mundane; it transcends to the metaphysical world, the world of universal ideas such as faith, love, courage, fear (Tompea), that all cultures have in common. Through them, our ancestors gave future generations something to hold onto when trying to understand their origins.

Ioana Corduneanu, co-author of "Semiotics of White Spaces on the Romanian Traditional Blouse, the *IA*," is a Romanian architect and founder of *Semne Cusute* (Sewn Signs), a blog transformed into an online community that strives to carry on *ia*'s legacy by bringing together people who are interested in the traditional methods of weaving and sewing. She outlines the semiotic structure of the traditional blouse; the most important motifs include celestial elements (suns, moons, stars, angels etc.), geometric elements (such as the diamond with seeds which represents the most popular symbol of fertility), and "The Rivers" which flow either straight or meandrous down the sleeve of the garment, depending on how the region's topography influences their course (Corduneanu and Dragan 54). When wearing the *ia*, a woman "carries the sky on her shoulders, the story of her past (origins and rituals) on the back of the garment, and the stories of the future (collective fears and beliefs) on the front" (Tompea). This is essential to know in a conversation on giving credit to folklore.

The outside world had no idea about our beloved *ia* before the French painter Henri Matisse acknowledged its existence in one of his Expressionist masterpieces "La Blouse Roumaine," in 1940. Since then, it has gained popularity on the international scene. The first notable designer who paid homage to the Romanian blouse is Yves Saint Laurent; he strongly promoted the apparel in his 1981 A/W collection dedicated to Matisse's "La Blouse Roumaine" (Tompea). *Ia* became a statement piece that never gets out of style, a must-have for every fashion connoisseur. While Romanians were enjoying the international recognition, a new issue came into sight. Some foreign fashion houses started taking advantage of the Romanian culture and made great profits from pieces that replicated the original source. This is the reason why Andreea Tanasescu, former casting director at MediaPRO Studios in Bucharest, decided to rise against injustice and founded *La Blouse Roumaine*, an online community that fights cultural appropriation of the Romanian blouse, aiming to transform *ia* into a national brand. In an interview she gave in June 2020 to Mihnea Maruta, journalist and host of *InspiraTIFF*, she recalls the scandal caused by Tory Burch that claimed one of her 2017 coats was inspired from the African culture but emulated on a one-to-one scale a Romanian Coat exhibited at the Metropolitan Museum of Art. The online community's followers, as Tanasescu recounts, stormed on Tory Burch's social media pages, and demanded the brand to admit the real inspiration for the 2017 collection—which they did in less than 48 hours while also removing the clothing items from their line.

Another incident that occurred around the same time tarnished Christian Dior's reputation. Tanasescu states that she recognized two embroidered vests that perfectly resembled the traditional vest from the historical region of Bukovina, Northern Romania, with prices starting at $30,000 in Dior's 2017 collection. After the Tory Burch fuss, *La Blouse Roumaine* was already set on proposing a bill that would protect Romanian folk symbols from being misused—and what Dior did was the last straw (Tanasescu).

Even though the copyright bill didn't pass through, Tanasescu started the #GiveCredit campaign with a similar aim: raising awareness over copyrights and intellectual property theft of unregulated artistic creations such as the folk costumes. She said she was motivated to create this campaign because the traditional weaving techniques and motifs should not be appropriated without acknowledging their origin. A further aim of all her actions would consist of bringing creative industries and local communities together to support the intangible Romanian heritage passed down through many generations. Tanasescu also initiated the Universal Day of the Romanian Blouse—with the help of the Embassy of Romania in Washington DC—which has been celebrated since 2013 on the 24th of June (Midsummer Day or *Sânziene*) in Romanian communities all over the world after being officially recognized by the Office of the Mayor of Washington, D.C.

Intellectual property theft has undergone a surge in the past few years due to the lack of copyright laws for apparel. While inspiration is understandable, plagiarism is not. And that's exactly what happened in both of the cases mentioned above. Amalia Sabiescu, author of "Problematizing heritage crafts authorship and ownership: steps towards the intellectual property protection of the traditional Romanian blouse," describes the authorship of heritage craft—which is essential when talking about intellectual property protection—as "collective and anonymous," fundamentally different from contemporary crafts (186). Thus, it is harder to exert the power of IP protection over artisans' work. Nowadays, the know-how of traditional crafts goes beyond households, into collective associations which support production that was once only practiced at home by peasant women (Sabiescu 186). This doesn't make authorship less important; on the contrary, unauthorized selling of knock-offs may be regarded as an ethical theft. But as of today, there is no international intellectual property law to safeguard these crafts.

For a Romanian woman, the *ia* has a story attached to it because of its symbolism given by our ancestors' centuries of labour and sweat. When I told my grandma about this media mess, she put her finger on it: "I'm happy they haven't gone through the horrors Mamma has in order to get the inspiration for my *hora* (Romanian folk circle dance) blouse."

Works Cited

Corduneanu, Ioana and Dragan, Nicolae-Sorin. "Semiotics of White Spaces on the Romanian Traditional Blouse, the *IA*." *Romanian Journal of Communication and Public Relations*, vol. 18, no. 3 (39), December 2016, pp. 49-63.

Fuciu, Maria. Personal interview. 4 December 2020

Gheorghiță, Lavinia. "Ia, or La Blouse Roumaine: Between Ethnicity and High-End Fashion." *RoDiscover*, 29 Oct. 2020, www.rodiscover.com/heritage/ia-or-la-blouse-roumaine-between-ethnicity-and-

       high-end-fashion.
Sabiescu, Amalia. "Problematising heritage crafts authorship and ownership: Steps towards the
       intellectual property protection of the traditional Romanian blouse." *Research Handbook on*
       Intellectual Property and Creative Industries, Edward Elgar Publishing, 2018, p. 186.
Tanasescu, Andreea Diana. "Episodul 5. Mihnea Maruta in dialog cu Andreea Diana Tanasescu." *TIFF*
       Unlimited season 1, 22 June 2020, www.unlimited.tiff.ro/inspiratiff/ season:1/videos/episodul-5-
       mihnea-maru-a-in-dialog-cu-andreea-diana-tanasescu.
Tompea, Roxana Claudia. "The #GiveCredit Campaign and Why It Matters: A Case Study of La blouse
       Roumaine." *International Journal of Fashion Design Technology and Education*, July 2020.

Honorable Mention—First-Year Writing

Mapping Essay—Build from your profile in Project Two to identify an associated area of intellectual curiosity or expertise. In Project Three, describe and explain a concept, controversy, or phenomenon connected to your area of interest. This project will require the skillful and informative use of at least two additional recent, relevant, reputable (primary or secondary) sources beyond those you used in Project Two. With this support in hand, you are to construct an essay—a map, if you will—orienting your readers to a significant aspect of the topic you have chosen.

—Dr. Deirdre McMahon

Caroline Gallen
Take Nothing So That You Can Have Everything

If you ever happen to find yourself in Newtown, Pennsylvania, I recommend paying a visit to Tyler State Park. Once you get to the park's central hub, known to locals as "the dam," go straight across the bridge and up a beaten, rocky trail until you reach your destination: a quaint yet sturdy wooden bridge crossing a shallow creek, covered in more doodles than a kindergartener's desk. The bridge has an official name, but most of the people I know call it "Boy Scout Bridge" since it was built by a local troop. This nature-worn structure secluded among the woods is an open invitation for passersby of all walks of life to write what is on their minds; the bridge's content varies from cheesy, cliché quotes like "when you travel, adventure finds you," to somber poems intermixed with assorted graffiti and funny, miscellaneous ramblings. At the top of the bridge, painted in bold, yellow capitals is the phrase "take nothing so you can have everything." I always liked to think that this phrase defined the therapeutic purpose of the bridge; people could step onto it, scrawl down any troubling thoughts they may have, and then move on with their hike, leaving behind the weight of a heavy mind as they cross the bridge to the other side.

One chilly fall day, I made the ever-familiar trek to the bridge with a goal in mind: to document as much of the bridge's art as possible. By the time I reached the end of the bridge, I had taken over 40 pictures, each offering a glimpse into the writer's life in that snapshot in time. I saw a pattern that saddened me yet did not shock me; there were many indications that most of the writings were done by adolescents, whether it was the sloppy handwriting, subject matter, or flat-out stating of their age. These writings too often reflected feelings of confusion, hopelessness, and pain, the same emotions that define the "angsty teen" stereotype that many adults use to invalidate the genuine conflicts that people my age experience. I have heard my fair share of patronizations throughout my years: "you're just a kid, you don't know what's good for you," "stop being so dramatic," and "your problems mean nothing."

Hearing from the adults in their life that their feelings are frivolous and unimportant slowly withers away teens' willingness to share their thoughts. Nonetheless, these contemplations must be shared; they cannot be left inside, continuously building in pressure like an expanding gas until they burst their container. Hence the prevalence of adolescent writings on the Boy Scout Bridge, an anonymous form of confiding one's thoughts to a medium that listens and does not judge or scold them.

There is a growing need for safe communicative spaces for teens; according to the 2019 Youth Risk Behavior Survey, the percentage of teens who "experienced persistent feelings of sadness or hopelessness" increased by 10.6% over the span of a decade, from 26.1% in 2009 to 36.7% in 2019 (Centers for Disease Control and Prevention). In other words, American teens are experiencing increasing difficulty in their transition from childhood to adulthood. This concerning trend raises an important follow-up question: how are these depressed, "angsty" youths dealing with their feelings? The ideal situation for these adolescents would be to confide in their adult guardians; indeed, "youth who feel connected at school and at home were found to be as much as 66% less likely to experience health risk behaviors related to sexual health, substance use, violence, and mental health in adulthood" (Steiner et al). Through this sense of "connectedness," the adults that support a teen create a barrier between that blooming flower and the harsh, overwhelming elements that can beat it down. Teens that do not have this safeguard against the extremes of life are more likely to make destructive choices. Ultimately, the adults in the life of a teen impact that teen's regulation of his or her emotions by providing that essential communicative comfort; however, adolescents will find ways to express their whirlwinds of thoughts regardless of adult support, because to do otherwise could lead to explosion.

First-Year Writing | 25

These are the authors of the Boy Scout Bridge. One kid was "overthinking it" when he or she visited the bridge. Another wrote that "when you are young, they assume you know nothing," a possible jab at the figures in this teen's life that dismiss his or her thoughts. This sense of dismissal is not isolated: yet another wrote "I'm only 17 I don't know anything." Maybe this is not entirely false; it is true that, in comparison to their adult guardians, teens have less life experience. However, does this naivety justify the dismissal of an adolescent's feelings? If anything, it calls for the opposite; adults have the privilege of perspective, whereas teens do not. Lacking life experience puts teens at a disadvantage when handling their reactions to a situation, since they do not have previous experiences with which to compare novel ones. Additionally, regions of teens' brains develop at different rates; the amygdala, an area that governs intense, primal emotions such as fear and anger, develops faster than the prefrontal cortex, the center of logic, decision-making, and emotion regulation ("Brain Development: Teenagers"). In fact, many adolescents are well into adulthood before their critical thinking regions are fully formed ("Brain Development: Teenagers"). This difference in developmental rates can create a frustrating discrepancy between a teen's emotions and his or her ability to reason with and handle those emotions.

This newness to different life events combined with a still-developing prefrontal cortex creates intense emotions that can overwhelm adolescents. Knowing this, I am inclined to believe that the author of a particularly somber, weather-worn poem that caught my eye on one of the bridge's posts is a teenager. (For the ease of narration, I am going to refer to the author as a teenage male, since my first impression from seeing the poem's handwriting was that it looked like male handwriting). Due to the age of the poem and its survival through possibly months of rain, snow, and heat, it is difficult to read in its entirety. However, certain lines or words jump out to indicate that the author's romantic interest broke up with him, a highly emotionally charged event that can be especially difficult if it is the author's first ended relationship. So why write such a personal, gut-wrenching note for strangers to read? Chances are, this teen was hesitant to expose this side of himself to the adults in his life for fear of receiving likely well-intentioned but condescending comfort. "Wait until you get to college, there's plenty of people to date there," does not provide any solace to a high schooler who has not yet experienced college nor its rich social environment. Everything that the author knows lies in the present; he is upset that his relationship is over, and the magnitude of this loss feels particularly heavy if it is his first. Perhaps to avoid being talked down upon, as well as any conflicts that may arise from the generational miscommunication between him and his guardians, this boy decided to write his anguish on the bridge, where passersby cannot judge him based on his age, and instead only pity him for his words.

This hypothetical heartbroken teen boy is just one example of many who use the Boy Scout Bridge as an outlet for their grief. Although it is sad to see physical manifestations of teens struggling with their mental health, there is hope written on the bridge as well. In addition to realizing they are not alone in their struggles by seeing what others have written, adolescents are also offered words of comfort; one passerby wrote "You are loved" near the teen who "doesn't know anything." Another crossed out a gay slur and affirmed that "this bridge is NOT homophobic." Yet another professed "Fate is not absolute" and that they "believe in the good of humanity." After seeing all the positive and encouraging messages responding to the negative ones, I think I believe in the good of humanity too. Despite possibly not receiving support at home, teens can still receive some much-needed reassurance from strangers on the bridge. As the number of teens reporting mental health issues continues to rise, I expect to see more somber writings on Boy Scout Bridge. However, I also expect a rise in uplifting notes; if guardians and educators fail to acknowledge this mental health crisis among the American youth and install programs to combat its rise, then the locals of Tyler State Park will step up to do what we can to support those who hike to the Boy Scout Bridge. In the end, everyone deserves to travel lightly and take nothing with them as they move throughout life, free from heavy thoughts and free to explore the everything of their future.

Works Cited

"Brain Development: Teenagers." *Raising Children Network,* 1 July 2020, raisingchildren.net.au/pre-teens/development/understanding-your-pre-teen/brain-development-teens.

Centers for Disease Control and Prevention, *Youth Risk Behavior Survey Data Summary and Trends Report 2009 2019,* www.cdc.gov/healthyyouth/data/yrbs/pdf/YRBSDataSummaryTrends Report 2019-508.pdf.

Steiner, Riley J., et al. "Adolescent Connectedness and Adult Health Outcomes." *American Academy of Pediatrics,* American Academy of Pediatrics, July 2019, pediatrics. aappublications. org/content/144/1/e20183766.

Honorable Mention—First-Year Writing

For this assignment, you may choose to write in either of two genres: literacy narrative or memoir.

—Dr. Sheila Sandapen

Sanjana Suresh
The Last Dance

"Performing her last item, the Varnam, please welcome back to the stage Sanjana Suresh!" The MC's voice boomed through two enormous speakers that occupied either side of the surprisingly massive Crossroads North Middle School auditorium stage. A cool breeze rushed into the backstage area and I turned around to see a huge black door left ajar. Just outside the door, orange leaves were swept up by gusts of wind as the late October evening settled in. The sight calmed me as I turned back around to face the stage and attempted to even out my breathing.

"This is it," I thought to myself, taking everything in with a deep breath. My feet were throbbing after dancing for two and a half hours, but I ignored the pain. In the split second I had before I took my last steps onto the daunting stage, memories from the past year flooded my brain. Right when my dance teacher, Balaakka, uttered the words, "your Arangetram is set for October 28th, 2017," I embarked on an intense journey. I started preparing for my Arangetram an entire year in advance. I knew the gravity of having an Arangetram, since Balaakka stressed its importance to me every week when I went to her house for dance class throughout the nine years that I was her student.

"It is not just an Indian classical dancer's graduation from our wonderful art form, Bharathanatyam," Balaakka would say, "but it is also a dancer's solo debut on stage in front of hundreds of friends and family members. You will be performing for three hours all alone up on that stage. There is no room for mistakes."

When I first started learning Bharathanatyam as a young girl, I always viewed an Arangetram as some far away, insurmountable event that was purely hypothetical. Whenever the older girls in my class were preparing for their Arangetrams, I would listen to the conversations that they had with Balaakka.

"You will have three costume changes, so make sure you tell me what colors you want your costumes to be ahead of time," Balaakka would say, "and please do not forget to have your speech and your parents' speeches approved by me. This will be the biggest event of your life, even your wedding will not be as stressful!"

I never really thought about myself going through the vigorous Arangetram prepping process until reality set in when Balaakka announced the date of my Arangetram and I knew I had to get serious. I knew that every day of practice I could get until the day of my Arangetram was crucial. I knew that there were thousands of dollars and hours being put into my performance. I knew that this journey would not be easy. However, I was determined to get through the year and overlook all of the pressure not only to prove to myself that I could take on such a challenge, but to see my parents beam at me with pride while watching me dance on stage.

And that's exactly what I did. I got through the year smoothly. Until September.

Once September rolled around, I was a sophomore at South Brunswick High School. Sophomore year was easily the worst year of high school I experienced because I decided to take all Honors classes, and at South Brunswick High School, Honors classes are notorious for having a great deal of coursework. On top of that, I had to practice tirelessly for my Arangetram for at least four hours a day during the first two months of the school year. To say those two months were rough is truly an understatement. Even after getting home from school and starting my homework immediately, I was unable to finish everything I needed to do before 11 p.m. Though I was drained from school and homework, I had to push myself and practice the eight pieces that I was expected to perform at my Arangetram.

By the time I finished practicing it was 2 a.m. Every night.

Yet, I still woke up for school at 6 a.m. The cycle was vicious, but I knew it had to be done. I struggled to stay awake in my classes. My bloodshot eyes, callused feet, and aching arms were begging me to stop for the entirety of the two months that I pushed my limits. Even my parents questioned my sanity when they heard the daily rhythmic thudding of my feet against the cold, white tiles in our basement well past midnight. I never truly grasped the idea of perseverance until my head felt as though it was on fire from the lack of sleep, and my legs were practically giving out, but I still practiced diligently as if my life depended on it because in the moment, it did.

The meaning of my Arangetram went way beyond just me dancing on stage. It was a microcosm to my life as a whole. My parents immigrated to the United States from India years before I was born just so that they could provide my sister and me with lives they could only dream of in the small village where they came from. My parents never wanted to explicitly detail out their struggles to me, but Balaakka immigrated to the United States from India too, and she had a lot to openly say about it.

"Sanjana, you truly do not realize how lucky you kids are these days," Balaakka would ramble, "back in India, we had to walk miles and miles and catch multiple buses just to get to school every day. Everything is so easily accessible for you kids here in America. That's why your parents came here. I know they lived comfortably in India, but the opportunities in America are unmatched. I want you to understand and appreciate the sacrifices they made for you."

And that's exactly what I did.

Balaakka's words continuously circulated through my mind. She unveiled a new perspective that made me carry myself with humility and view my parents in a new light. I can only imagine how difficult the transition from

India to the United States was for my parents, but despite that notion, they never outwardly displayed their homesickness. Instead, their homesickness shone through dishes filled with South Indian spices made daily by my mom and various tunes sung by my dad's favorite South Indian singers that poured through our home's sound system. With this added perspective, I knew that my Arangetram was a big deal for my parents, but I still did not truly understand why.

Until I saw it.

I was about to conclude my Arangetram with my showstopping, 20-minute finale: the Varnam. I snapped out of my thoughts and walked onto the stage, following the rhythm of the beat that played faintly through the speakers. I caught sight of both of my parents in the front row of the audience. Their faces glimmered under traces of the spotlight that spilled onto them. My dad looked fancy in a navy-blue suit that was complemented by a bright red tie. My mom looked elegant in a light-green and violet patterned saree draped over her left shoulder. Looking at them, I knew that their suppressed homesickness had vanished, because standing in front of them in a traditional Indian classical costume with golden jewelry adorning my body from head to toe, I was their home. I embodied their home. They were certainly beaming at me with pride, which I wanted all along, but there was something more to it. That's when I saw it.

"I made it."

These words were written in their expressions. I could see it as clear as day through their smiles that were bigger than ever and the tears of joy that made their eyes glisten. The revelation overwhelmed me with happiness that I was unable to mask on stage as I smiled right back at them. In that moment, I realized that my Arangetram was far more symbolic than simply a graduation from Bharathanatyam. My Arangetram signified that my parents truly made it. They immigrated to the United States with barely any money in their pockets and hardly any support from people in their village. My parents' neighbors in India disapproved of their move to the United States because they claimed that my sister and I would grow up "uncultured" and "have no bone in our body that worked hard." When considering all of this, it became evident why my parents had this expression on their faces. Standing up on that stage, I was living proof to them and to everyone that doubted them that their sacrifices meant something. Their daughter, born in America, grew up so deeply connected to her Indian culture through Bharathanatyam. She was able to learn the art form for nine years and perform on stage in front of hundreds of people for three consecutive hours. She made this happen through her hard work. She is a true Bharathanatyam dancer, no matter where she is from.

That one look on my parents' faces was all I needed to persist through the last and longest piece of my Arangetram. Luckily, I started the Varnam off with my back turned to the audience for eight counts. I took those eight counts to briefly recuperate from my deep thoughts and get into the zone. At that point, my one and only goal was to blow the audience away. I wanted the last dance to convey to everyone what hard work and perseverance looked like. I wanted the last dance to leave everyone speechless and result in a standing ovation. But most importantly, I wanted the last dance to show everyone that although I am a South Asian American, I am very much connected to and passionate about my Indian culture.

    And that's exactly what the last dance did.

Honorable Mention—First-Year Writing

Evaluating and Solving Problems: For this assignment, you will research a problematic issue, propose one or more solutions to the problem, and present an argument supporting your solution. One effective way to approach this assignment is to identify a problem in a profession or discipline of interest to you. Another is to deal with a problem local to Drexel, Philadelphia, or your hometown, and relevant to your experience there. The topic should be original and significant.

—Professor Robert Finegan

Marie Ann Tomaj
Why are Females so Often Misdiagnosed?

For years, my sister struggled with severe menstrual pain. The pain was so debilitating that she couldn't move for days. My parents, concerned, took her to three different gynecologists, but they all deemed it normal. On January 2018, my sister visited the ER with abdominal pain and profuse vomiting. Without asking what she ate, the doctor determined it as food poisoning and gave her two Advil. After she became increasingly ill, he decided to conduct some additional tests. It was then determined that a ruptured cyst on her ovary was causing internal bleeding. Finally, after eleven years, she confirmed that the pain was not "normal" or "all in her head." She had been suffering from Polycystic Ovary Syndrome (PCOS) and surgery finally yielded an answer.

With all the technological and medical advances in the 21st century, one would think that a misdiagnosis would be minimal, but that is not the case. A new study at the University of Leeds explained that "Women have a 50 percent higher chance than men of receiving the wrong initial diagnosis following a heart attack" (Gale). A national survey on the challenges of communicating endometriosis pain done by Dr Stella Bullo, a lecturer in Linguistics at Manchester Metropolitan University, UK, found that 1 in 10 women in the UK suffer from endometriosis, but it takes 7.5 years worldwide for a correct diagnosis (Bullo). According to the Women's Health Care of Princeton, PCOS "affects 5-10% of women of childbearing age," but "[w]omen may experience PCOS symptoms for years before discovering what's causing their problems" (Why Polycystic). This is a common issue amongst women and according to Maya Dusenbury, a former worker at the National Institute for Reproductive Health, it is because of the "knowledge gap" (Seegert).

The "knowledge gap" refers to the lack of female presence in research/clinical studies, leading to a lack of understanding of the female body. Since the male body was considered a standard in science, tests were conducted on them. Females of child-bearing age were discouraged from partaking in these trials as it could affect their fertility. Many scientists also refused to include females because of their hormonal inconsistencies, which they believed could negatively impact their results (Seegert). Because the knowledge of the female body was lacking, in 1993 Congress passed the NIH Revitalization Act, "a law mandating that women and minorities be included in clinical trials funded by the NIH" (Johnson). While there has been progress, Paula Johnson, a Women's Health professor at Harvard, explained that "medical research is too often flawed by its failure to examine sex differences" (Johnson). In a 2010 study done by Annaliese Beery, a Neuroscience professor at Smith College, and Irving Zucker, the two looked at sex bias in neuroscience and biomedical research. They found that sex bias in human trials is decreasing, however studies still fail to analyze the results by sex (Beery). This is an issue because men and women have different symptoms to the same diseases. Barbara Goff, MD, chair of obstetrics and gynecology at the University of Washington in Seattle, explained that "[t]he symptoms of ovarian cancer often mimic those of irritable bowel syndrome or ingestion, or they're attributed to menopause" (Carter). Therefore, women often don't get diagnosed with ovarian cancer on the first try.

The lack of research, or analysis by sex, leads to the "trust gap," as Dusenbury has dubbed it (Seegert). Because the symptoms don't match the textbook, doctors often misdiagnose females or write them off as psychiatric patients. This causes a "trust gap." Doctors think the female patients are overreacting while women feel as if they aren't being listened to (Shaw). In an article, Gina Shaw, a former writer of the National Association of Children's Hospitals and Related Institutions, talks about Katy Seppi's difficulty with menstrual pain and misdiagnosis. After two decades, she was diagnosed with endometriosis, a painful disorder where the tissue inside the uterus starts growing outside and can wrap around the fallopian tubes and ovaries. Shaw explains how medical "gaslighting" is commonly experienced by females in healthcare. Instead of doing tests, doctors tell patients that what they are experiencing is normal. When Seppi complained about pelvic pain now known to be caused by endometriosis, "the ER doctor just said that I was probably ovulating, and it was normal to have more pain with ovulation." Seppi's case highlights the common gender bias that women are "too emotional" or are more likely to "overreact," leading to them being written up as psychiatric cases, as it was "all in their heads" (Shaw). In a scholarly article written by Annie Lin, an Associate Professor in Preventive Medicine at Northwestern University, et al., a study was conducted to view the trust levels between primary doctors and women with and without PCOS. According to the results, women with PCOS are more likely to distrust their doctors because "they received limited informational support provided about specific PCOS issues" (Lin). This shows that the "trust gap" doesn't just apply to doctors. Women are starting to distrust the people whose job is to help them.

To solve this issue, changes must be implemented. Johnsons explained that medical research is too often flawed by its failure to examine sex differences" (Johnson). Therefore, clinical trials should focus on analyzing results by sex in order to reduce misdiagnosis. Doctors should also try to be more forthcoming because, as Shaw explained, women often feel gaslighted or not listened to when it comes to relaying their issues. But this isn't about giving more to women; this is about treating them equally. When my father visited the ER, he was taken immediately upon mentioning chest discomfort. They ran multiple tests, and it was concluded that he was experiencing elevated amounts of stress. My sister, however, was made to wait.

While she no longer struggles as much, I know she'll never forget the eleven years of uncertainty. And I'll never forget how on January of 2018 I almost lost a sister because someone didn't want to do their job.

Works Cited

Beery, A., & Zucker, I. (2011, January). "Sex bias in neuroscience and biomedical research." Retrieved October 07,2020,fromhttps://www.ncbi.nlm.nih.gov/pmc/articles/PMC3008499.

Bullo, S. (2019, February 19). "I feel I'm being stabbed by a thousand tiny men: The challenges of communicating endometriosis pain." Retrieved October 7, 2020, from https://journalssagepubcom. ezproxy2.library.drexel.edu/doi/full/10.1177/1363459318817943.

Carter, K. (2019, March 13). "The Horrifying Reasons Why Women Are Constantly Let Down by Their Doctors." Retrieved October 07, 2020, https://www. prevention.com/health/a26100121/misdiagnosed women.

Gale, C. (2016, August 26). "Heart attacks in women more likely to be missed." Retrieved October 07 2020, https://www.leeds.ac.uk/news/article/3905/heart attacks in women more likely to be missed.

Johnson, P. A., Fitzgerald, T., Salganicoff, A., Wood, S. F., & Goldstein, J. M. (2014). "Sex-Specific Medical Research: Why Women's Health Can't Wait." Retrieved October 7, 2020, from https://www. brighamandwomens.org/assets/bwh/womens-health/pdfs/ConnorsReportFINAL.pdf.

Lin, A., Bergomi, E., Dollahite, J., Sobal, J., Hoeger, K., & Lujan, M. (2018, August 1). "Trust in Physicians and Medical Experience Beliefs Differ Between Women With and Without Polycystic Ovary Syndrome." Retrieved October 07, 2020, from https:// www.ncbi.nlm.nih.gov/pmc/articles/PMC6101505.

Seegert, L. (2018, November 16). "Women more often misdiagnosed because of gaps in trust and knowledge." Retrieved October 07, 2020, from https://healthjournalism.org/blog/2018/11/women-more-often-misdiagnosed-because-of-gaps-in-trust-and-knowledge.

Shaw, G. (2018, June 08). "Why Women Struggle to Get The Right Diagnosis." Retrieved from https://www.webmd.com/women/news/20180607/why-women-are-getting-misdiagnosed.

"Why Polycystic Ovarian Syndrome Is Often Misdiagnosed." (n.d.). Retrieved October 07, 2020, from https://www.princetongyn.com/blog/why-polycystic-ovarian-syndrome-is-often-misdiagnosed.

Honorable Mention—First-Year Writing

Memoir or Literacy Narrative: For your first formal project, your goal is to relate a memoir or literacy narrative and its significance to an audience through the use of specific detail and insight. Your memoir/literacy narrative should center on a moment of learning, competency, or education that was unexpected, in or out of school.

—Dr. Deirdre McMahon

Bethany White
Teach

When children are young, they believe that the world loves and accepts them just the way they are. For most children, school is a place where this same comfort exists, where kids can be themselves and learn how to respect others. Something I learned at a very young age is that teachers are human; they have bias and prejudice like any other person. The issue is when they allow this prejudice to influence the way they teach their young, impressionable students.

When I was in the first grade, there was a time that I asked my teacher to go to the restroom. She said no, and that I could go after class. A few minutes later, one of my classmates asked to go, and they were allowed. After seeing this, I asked once more when my classmate came back if I could go to the bathroom. I received a no then as well. All throughout class, I saw other children go to the bathroom while I sat close to tears just wanting to go. My parents always taught me to be respectful, and not to talk back to adults. I tried one last time, and this time, my teacher threatened to move my clothes pin from the green square, to yellow because I was being difficult. So, I went home, in tears, to tell my parents. After a brief parent teacher conference, nothing changed.

Another occurrence I had was when I was a little older in the sixth grade. We were reading *Tom Sawyer* in English class, but I had finished the book a little earlier than my classmates. During quiet time we could either read our assigned book or work on something quietly, so I picked up the book I was reading for fun. Shortly after I started reading, my teacher came up to me and asked me why I was not reading the assigned book. My friends who sat a few feet away from me were also done the assigned reading and were doing math homework, but my teacher did not approach them. So, I told her I finished, and she simply laughed and told me to get to work. I did not know what to do. I was so confused about this interaction, I picked up *Tom Sawyer* and pretended to read while my teacher watched me for the rest of the class.

One of the last experiences I had was in eighth grade. This was a few days after the police had killed Freddie Gray, and there were riots in Baltimore city. My teacher was required by the school to talk about the riots and police brutality so the students would be informed, but she did not recount events in a formal matter. Instead, she went on a tangent about how Black Lives Matter is propaganda from the left. She ranted about how Freddie Gray was a criminal. At the end, she locked eyes with me. In that stare we had a silent conversation which said, "You will not step out of line." In that moment I was *scared*. That was when I realized I was not just a student; I was a *black* student in a racist school. Looking around the classroom, I realized that my peers were unfazed. Two boys were laughing in the back corner, one girl was doodling in her notes. It occurred to me then that they had most likely heard this spiel before, whether from parents or another teacher, and they simply *did not care*.

After middle school, instead of going to my zone high school I attended a magnet school for the arts. The first day of school, I recognized a change; I was no longer the only student of color in my class. Moreover, the teachers did not care what race their students were. We talked openly in class about the racial unrest in the country. Students were *actually* punished for spewing hate speech, rather than just receiving a tap on the wrist. I had grown so used to the sneers and the micro-aggressions that I no longer read them as offensive. As soon as I stopped hearing them, I realized how heavily they had weighed on me. At this new school, I learned that I was not the only student who had grown up with a target on their back, waiting for the teachers to take their shot. Friends of mine had been rejected from participating in student council, they had been sent home early because of a hairstyle, or they had been walking on eggshells their entire life simply because their teachers hated them for the color of their skin.

This was when I realized all the occasions where I was the singled out by my teacher irrationally weren't because I was doing something wrong, but because the color of my skin made them believe I was going to misbehave, even if that was completely unfounded. For the first thirteen years of my life I was the only black student in a multitude of classes, but that was not the issue. It was because of my teachers' prejudice that this tainted my education experience.

The problem with our American education system is that teachers tend to stray from simply teaching content. Instead, they teach their personal bias. They teach hate and ignorance. They teach malice and pain. They teach revenge against the innocent because that is what they were taught. By enacting these micro-aggressions, they invalidated my race, but they have also made me question my identity as a young African American citizen. These micro-aggressions are not "micro," they are just as painful as any physical assault. It is our duty to stop this personal bias from tainting young minds. It took me thirteen years to be able to think for myself after I wrestled free from the strong grip the adults in my life had on me. It is time to teach children respect and love. It is time to teach children compassion and kindness. It is time to teach equality.

Honorable Mention—First-Year Writing

For this assignment, you may choose to write in either of two genres: literacy narrative or memoir. Please review the "Literacy Narrative" and "Memoir" chapters in *The Norton Field Guide*, choose the genre you would prefer to try, and write a draft due in class in week 3. Members of the class will share their ideas, and the final version will be due in the drop box in week 4.

—Dr. Fred Siegel

Cianni Williams
Corkscrew Curls

Phase One: The Straightening

The familiar, stingy smell hung over my nose as the uncomfortable blaze started on my roots. Pungent clouds full of smoke and hairspray fill the already too small spaces between clients. I sat in the second to last row, facing what looked like a foreign invader seeking Earth's leader. Four chunks of silver aluminum pieces clamped down on my fluffy cloud of hair.

"Alright baby, keep this in your hair for about 30 minutes, and then we will wash again." The soft soothing voice coming from Monica, my barely 5'2" hairdresser, contrasted with the harsh burning sensation that was taking over my scalp.

Guiding me over to the row of dryer chairs, she placed me on the end and lowered the heavy dome over my head. With a turn of a knob, more heat came onto my head. Sauna-like temperatures combatted with the chemical induced heat on top of my head, making it feel as though I would sweat my curls out before the chemicals did it.

While sitting in my hot spot, Spanish words swarm around me like a bustling hive full of bees. Gossip and petty laced words flew over my head, stinging just as much as the chemicals on top of my head.

"No me diga."

"Ah si."

"Ay dios mi."

Tapping my shoulder and bringing me back to my oven like reality, Monica's short frame stood over me. "You're done. Let's go wash."

As she lowered my head down into the bowl, I instantly felt the relief of the cool water extinguishing the flames on my head, taking out some of the curls along with it.

You have to do this. You have to change. It'll be easier.

Once all the solution was fully washed and rinsed out of my hair, Monica led me back over to her chair, and delicately placed each of her styling tools one by one in front of me. As she placed them, I felt that the hot implements were whispering to me, stating how they would make me look better.

Once Monica was satisfied with how my hair dried, she took the hot iron and began to change my hair. With each pass of the hot tool, it felt as though it was burning off every insult that entangled itself within my thick curls.

You would look so much better with your hair done. *Tsss.*

Do something with this mess. *Tsss.*

Your hair is uncontrollable. *Tssss.*

You ugly mutt. *Tsssssss.*

"Mami, you like it?" Monica gleefully asked, bumping out the sleek ends so they flow effortlessly down my shoulders. The once buoyant and springy ringlets now laid so vertically and unmoving.

"Yeah," I softly muttered, "I barely look like myself."

Phase Two: The Cutting

I'm done.

Tears forming hot puddles in the edges of my eyes as I stare at the unkempt and unevenness of my hair textures. It's been two good years with this struggle, feeling as though I was living as someone else. Asking myself almost every day if this is truly me. *How can I be the real me when my hair isn't even in its natural state?*

Grasping onto the heterogeneous parts of my hair, where the waves crashed into the harsh land, where the real me ends.

As the blade glided over the smooth strand, it offered no hesitation to my trembling fingers.

Snip.

In a split second, the lifeless strand laid motionless on the cold tiles of my bathroom floor.

"What. The. Hell?!"

My mother's face, tightening with confusion and stress, could barely make out the next few yells at me. Tears falling from their home, I stood there riddled with fear of what comes next. Instantly grabbing the scissors from my fingertips, my mother scanned over me, looking for a fitting punishment or a way to soothe my unseen pain.

"Come on," she finally broke the standoff, "We're getting you a haircut. Meet me in the car in 10 minutes." With that, my mother left the small bathroom with the speed of a swift feather.

Turning back to my mad reflection, I could only smile.

Finally. Me.

Phase Three: The Accepting

I stare at my reflection of small coffee colored ringlets that crowd my hair. Twisting and spiraling all over my head, my hair stands drastically changed from my breakdown four years prior. That day now felt like a small blemish in my history.

With the beginning of high school, I made the clear decision to start naturally and authentically. No more lies and artificial changes to myself. I was going to be me, and that truly started with my hair. I walked into my high school with a bushel of small buds on top of my head, ready to show the world my curls' potential.

I once heard that your hair is like your little garden; you give it some love, and it'll grow with so much beauty. I smile, twirling one small soft corkscrew curl. "Just give it some love, and it'll grow."

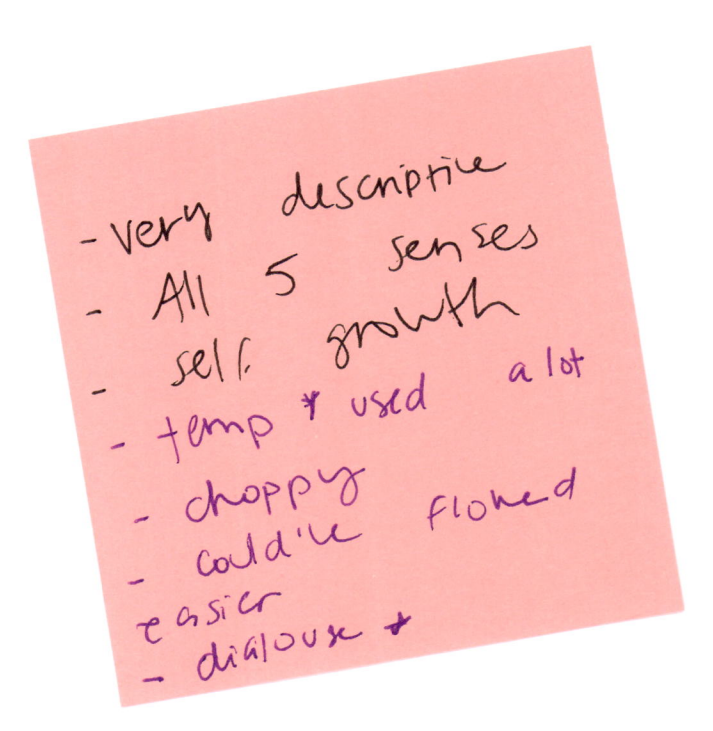

- very descriptive
- All 5 senses
- self growth
- temp * used a lot
- choppy
- could've flowed easier
- dialouge *

Drexel Publishing Group

Essays

Introduction

Researching, thinking, and writing are at the core of the College of Arts and Sciences. In every field, students must be able to find and evaluate the best evidence and information on a topic. Students must be able to form original ideas, and then write with a fresh approach.

The following essays were selected from student submissions to the Drexel Publishing Group Essay Contest. The contest was judged by faculty from a wide range of disciplines in the College of Arts and Sciences. The essays in this section of *The 33rd* explore diverse topics such as gender roles, elections, the environment, education, and literature. These student writers demonstrate originality, nuance, and passion, and do so in a variety of disciplines in the arts and sciences.

To honor the stylistic requirements of each field, we have reproduced the essays and articles in their original forms.

—*The Editors*

First Place—Humanities

Gabrielle Werner

Frankenstein, Scientific Advancement, and the God Complex

Victor Frankenstein's journey to the creation of life in *Frankenstein* is often seen as an example of a scientist with a god complex. This pursuit is a kind of forbidden knowledge along the lines of Agrippa and Paracelsus' works that crosses a moral line in scientific advancement. Frankenstein specifically, however, did not have a god complex because his focus was on discovery and not power, and he considered the negative consequences for his actions even before he was affected personally. By giving life to his monster, Frankenstein does resemble a godlike figure, but he never wanted to be like a god, and was instead obsessed with achieving a never-before-seen scientific discovery that other scientists found impossible.

Frankenstein is often seen as a prominent example of a scientist with a god complex. The idea of the god complex is commonly applied to scientists that go too far in experiments with no regard for morality or the consequences for their actions. It is characterized by inflated feelings of arrogance, infallibility, and lack of empathy. *Frankenstein* is a stigma among scientists for its depiction of the negative consequences of scientific advancement, with Dr. Frankenstein representing the mad scientist with a god complex and the destruction that results from his endeavors (Nagy 1143). Frankenstein himself even resembles a god in the act of the creation of life. He creates a creature that ends up being the ugliness of his inner self-given life, just as God made man in his image. Frankenstein takes on the mad scientist archetype in his pursuit of a breakthrough, devoting himself so completely to his work that he is consumed by it, able to do nothing else (Nagy 1147). He is one of many fictional scientists that goes too far and ends up being the cause of the death of his loved ones.

Dr. Frankenstein, however, does not really have the typical god complex seen among mad scientist types. At a basic level, he doesn't even view himself as a scientist, and is never referred to as such. He is a student making discoveries and trying to learn more about how the world works. He is driven by the desire to do something new, which is why he chose to study science: "In other studies you go as far as others have gone before you, and there is nothing more to know; but in a scientific pursuit there is continual food for discovery and wonder" (Shelley 51-52). Despite his multiple breakthroughs in his studies, he is not actually referred to as a scientist because the terminology did not exist yet at the time that the novel was written (Nagy 1145). Frankenstein thus becomes an early conceptualization for scientists, for better or worse, which contributes to widespread fear over scientific advancement in unknown fields that seem to be fonts of "forbidden" knowledge. Frankenstein's status as a student rather than a scientist in his conception of himself is significant to his lack of a god complex in that it emphasizes his desire to learn and make his mark in the form of a significant advancement without the hubris later associated with the typical mad scientist.

The image of the scientist that later results from the mad scientist stereotype built around Frankenstein is unaware of the dangers of their work. Frankenstein, in his years spent creating his monster, doesn't consider the implications of what he is doing as he is completely engrossed by the idea of the project itself. As he is the first to make this discovery, there is no precedent for the morality of the situation. However, there are dangers in the pursuit of scientific discovery, and Frankenstein falls into the category of being unaware of the dangers of his creation because he is set in his belief of his work being for the greater good. Science is a "two-headed force: its potential for good is matched by its potential for destruction" (Nagy 1145). Though the creature ended up being highly destructive, Frankenstein's intentions were to advance science for the good of the many. Intentions make a big difference for someone like Frankenstein. While the typical mad scientist with a god complex is incredibly focused on the self and the potential benefits they will receive from their experiments, Frankenstein's aim wasn't selfish. He intended to uncover the secrets of life which could be used for the good of many, and did not consider that he was making something that could act as a servant to him or that he could potentially use his understanding of the nuances of life and death to bring his mother back. Though he was unaware of the dangers, he was also unaware of the ways in which he could take advantage of his discovery.

Going along with the idea of science's potential for good and destruction being evil, Frankenstein exists between these two potentials in a liminal state like his narrative inspiration, Prometheus. Liminal literally means "on the threshold," and it refers to the state one exists in between two worlds, as in a rite of passage. Prometheus is a liminal trickster existing between the worlds of gods and men that uses his existence in this state to steal fire from the gods for the humans. *Frankenstein* is also known as *The Modern Prometheus* because the pursuit of scientific discovery is likened to Prometheus and the fire. The images of fire and reanimation throughout *Frankenstein* act as reference to the story of Prometheus (Tudor 122). Frankenstein is a Prometheus-like figure not only because he is undone by his advancement but also because he exists in a liminal state between "good" and "bad." His intentions for his discoveries to be used for the greater good are matched by his creature's destruction. While the story of *Frankenstein* can serve as a warning against the subversion of morals in scientific advancement, it can also be a celebration of ambition for the benefit of others over the self.

Dr. Frankenstein did not consider ethics or morality in his creation of life, which is one of the main reasons he is widely considered a scientist with a god complex. Disregard for morals is what drives the archetypal mad scientist to go too far in their experiments, and this is a category that Frankenstein falls into. However, this disregard only goes as far as the completion of the experiment. Because Frankenstein is so driven by his ambition in discovering the secret of life and achieving something new, there are many aspects of his actions that he does not consider (Peterfreund 80-81). Once the creature is born, an awareness for what he has done comes crashing down on him. In other words, once the hypothetical became reality, he began to consider things he hadn't before. Unlike the mad scientist with a god complex, Frankenstein then gives up on all scientific pursuits, rather than continuing in his experiments with life or trying to perfect his form of creation. He also later takes responsibility for the destruction he was wrought by refusing to make a companion for the creature and chasing it to the ends of the earth to kill it. If he had a god complex, he would have continued his experiments until he was personally faced with negative consequences without regard for morals, but, since he is instead driven by ambition, the moment where he finally achieved something not thought to be possible snapped him out of his mad scientist processes.

Though Frankenstein is likened to a god by his act of creation, he never wanted to be a creator. Again, he did not consider the reality of what he was doing beyond making new discoveries, so he did not even realize that he was acting as a god. His immediate rejection of the creature shows a lack of a creator's love and benevolence. Though the creature was made in Frankenstein's image, it is not the beauty of man but rather the ugliness of Frankenstein's inner self, and this makes Frankenstein reject him. "Cursed creator! Why did you form a monster so hideous that even you turned from me in disgust? God in pity made man beautiful and alluring, after his own image; but my form is a filthy type of yours, more horrid from its very resemblance" (Shelley 133). It isn't until the creature comes to him and tells his story that Frankenstein realizes he is a creator, a god, with a responsibility to his creation (Tudor 127). The rejection of the creature is not only a rejection of the thing he has created, but also a rejection of himself as a creator. The darkest part of himself that the creature represents, the person that wasted away in his lab, that spent too much time at graveyards and watching the dead decay, is something that he did not want to become. Though Frankenstein represents a godlike figure with the power to create life, he doesn't truly have a god complex because he didn't think of the realities of his experiment and had no desire to be the master of something in creating life.

Frankenstein's most prominent moment in subverting the god complex is his refusal to give life to another creature despite the threat on his family. Frankenstein was ready to appease the creature by creating a companion in order to make them go away, never to be seen again. Though he understood that his act of creation was unnatural and negligent, he would have created another if it meant being able to ignore the realities of what he had done (Tudor 126). However, as this was his second time creating life, he was already attuned to what his end product would be and was affected differently. When it came down to it, Frankenstein couldn't create this companion for his creature because he couldn't escape this new creature's potential for destruction. The mad scientist's consumption with his work was gone, and not only did Frankenstein think of the morality of this situation, he also thought about what he would be inflicting on humanity. A true mad scientist with a god complex would make that second creature because he has the capabilities, and he could only be benefitted by the promise that he personally would never have to see them again. Frankenstein finally takes responsibility for his actions by refusing to be complacent.

A typical aspect of the god complex is a disinterest with societal consequences (Nagy 1145). Frankenstein, in creating his monster, is only concerned with his idea of "the greater good" in uncovering the secrets of life and doesn't consider the dangers. However, after his experiment is complete, he moves away from this and thus rejects the idea of the god complex. He feels incredible guilt over the deaths that result from his creation, as if he had killed them with his own hands. He does everything he can to try and save Justine from being executed for William's murder. This guilt is absent from the idea of the mad scientist, as they focus on the boons of their experiments and not the harm that will result unless they are affected personally. Frankenstein's refusal to create a companion for his creature also shows his consideration for societal consequences. Though he may not have been personally affected since the creature swore to stay away from him, he had no idea if this new creature would try to hurt people or if his first creature would break his promise of pacifism, and he couldn't abide by this potential for the destruction of humanity even if it was out of his sight.

Comparatively, Frankenstein as a mad scientist with a god complex is more human than other fictional scientists falling into this category. Other notable examples of the mad scientist in literature can be found in Nathaniel Hawthorne's "The Birthmark" and "Rappaccini's Daughter." "The Birthmark" depicts a mad scientist experimenting on his wife to remove a birthmark from her face and make her perfect but ends up killing her in the process. *Frankenstein* connects to this through the rejection of what the scientist considers ugly and the scientist's overwhelming obsession. The mad scientist in "Rappaccini's Daughter" experiments with poisonous plants and inadvertently turns his daughter into a kind of poisonous plant through her constant exposure to poison. Frankenstein's experiment also ends up hurting the people he loves, killing them through his negligence. In both stories, the scientist loses his loved ones because he has gone too far in his experiments. They represent the mad scientist with a god complex because their hubris keeps them from realizing their mistakes until it's too late, and their loved ones get hurt through their lack of regard for morality and ethics. In comparison to these mad scientists, Frankenstein appears as a more human scientist with closer consideration for the consequences of his actions and foray into what is considered forbidden knowledge. Frankenstein does not directly involve his family and friends in his experiments, and instead tries to keep them as far from it as possible. When he could have used his understanding of the secrets of life to try to bring his mother back to life, he never even considered it. Though many people close to him do end up getting hurt because of his creation, he realized his mistakes before that point. He regretted what he had done immediately, even before he was personally affected by the negative consequences of his actions. He rejected science completely and resolved himself to focus on other pursuits. Frankenstein's actions immediately following the success of his experiment show his desire for advancement as a student instead of the hubris of a scientist with a god complex, and thus humanizes him over what can be seen in other stories of mad scientists that don't realize they've gone too far until it's too late.

Frankenstein at its core is a story about the inevitability of scientific advancement. Dr. Frankenstein's overwhelming drive in completing his experiment in order to make a never-before-seen discovery shows what possesses scientists in performing experiments despite questions of ethics, which is especially important in a modern world. The stigma around what is considered to be Frankenstein's god complex is used as justification for a fear of science (Nagy 1146). Today, as fields like artificial intelligence and robotics advance, science poses a threat to the established status quo. There could possibly be a major shift in society with these developments, and a story like Frankenstein's about the dangers of unchecked experimentation can be seen as a justification for conservativism in sciences (Nagy 1152). Science, however, is an integral part of our lives, and progress cannot be halted by a desire to avoid change. Though questions on morality need to be asked in order to avoid unethical experimentation and development, the stigma of the god complex resulting from Frankenstein's monster is simply fearmongering to prevent societal change and is unreliable in a real-world discussion of scientific advancement.

Though *Frankenstein* is often discussed as the story of a mad scientist with a god complex, particularly one of the first mad scientists with a god complex, a deeper analysis of the particulars of what it means to have a god complex and Frankenstein's actions beyond his act of creation show that, while he becomes like a god through creating life, he does not actually have a god complex. Frankenstein is simply a student trying to make his mark by discovering something that was thought to be impossible. His consideration for others beyond how it affects himself and his rejection of the idea of being a master in creating life make him more human than the stereotypical mad scientist. The idea of Frankenstein having a god complex is used as justification for fear of scientific advancement, when in reality scientific advancement that has proper consideration for ethics and morality should be encouraged as advancement is as inevitable as the pursuit of knowledge.

Works Cited

Nagy, Peter, et al. "Why Frankenstein is a Stigma Among Scientists." *Sci Eng Ethics*, vol. 24, 2017, pp. 1143-1159.

Peterfreund, Stuart. "Composing What May Not Be 'Sad Trash': A Reconsideration of Mary Shelley's Use of Paracelsus in *Frankenstein*." *Studies in Romanticism*, vol. 43, no. 1, 2004, pp. 79–98.

Shelley, Mary. *Frankenstein*. 1818. Penguin Classics, 2013.

Tudor, Lucia-Alexandra. "Frankenstein: the myth of dark creation." *Romanian Journal of Artistic Creativity*, vol. 1, no. 3, 2013, p. 113-151.

Second Place—Humanities

Vivek Babu
The Television and The American Dream

Amy Tan's "Two Kinds" explores Jing-mei Woo's painful childhood as she and her mother attempt to achieve the American Dream. For Jing-mei's mother, the American Dream is the belief that individuals who work hard are entitled to success and upward social mobility. Tan uses the symbol of the television to highlight how the American Dream evolves: while it once remained a symbol of hopeful optimism for Jing-mei's future, the Dream quickly turns into a nightmare as Jing-mei and her mother realize that the American success they craved was unattainable.

Initially, the television is used as a lens through which Jing-mei's mother sees the American Dream. When Mrs. Woo believes that Jing-mei could be the next "Chinese Shirley Temple," they begin studying Shirley Temple's mannerisms, as though they are "watching training films" (Tan). Immediately, the television symbolizes their belief that the only way to achieve success in America was not through discovering Jing-mei's individuality, but by imitating the fame of established celebrities. Jing-mei and her mother's perception of the Dream is rooted in their longing for other people's success. Moreover, the hopeful mirage of the American Dream is shown through the symbol of Shirley Temple. Receiving Hollywood success at five years old, Shirley Temple was a key icon of the Great Depression by being able to reassure movie audiences that the depression would end and their bright futures were nearing (Desowitz). By directly comparing Jing-mei to Shirley Temple, Jing-mei is pressured to not only achieve fame at such a young age, but also liberate her family from their poor socioeconomic conditions.

However, in practice, Mrs. Woo's dream of turning her daughter into Shirley Temple quickly fades away when Jing-mei tries to get Shirley Temple's iconic curly haircut. As Jing-mei emerges with "an uneven mass of crinkly, black fuzz," her mother laments the mess of her hair, acting as if Jing-mei had done this on purpose (Tan). When Jing-mei fails to live up to the expectations created by the television, Mrs. Woo's instinct is to blame her daughter, refusing to acknowledge that Shirley Temple had far greater resources and opportunities to become successful. Expecting the same results in vastly different socioeconomic conditions, the flaws of the American Dream become apparent. This blind optimism that hard work directly translates into success minimizes the effects that privilege has in achieving greater social mobility. For Jing-mei to become the "next Chinese Shirley Temple," Jing-mei and her mother would have to overcome vastly different barriers as a poor Chinese immigrant compared to a middle-class white girl (Tan). Thus, the television is used to symbolize the illusion of the American Dream, as it became the only frame through which Mrs. Woo envisions her daughter's success.

This symbolism is extended through the dynamic of Mrs. Woo and her broken television. Jing-mei observes that while watching *The Ed Sullivan Show*, every time her mother sat down, the television would go silent (Tan).

But as soon as her mother got "halfway up the sofa to adjust the set," the sound would come back on (Tan). Mrs. Woo's control of the television symbolizes the constant attention that she had put toward Jing-mei's future. Unable to passively drive her daughter to conform to her expectations of hard work, Mrs. Woo is forced to actively interfere with Jing-mei's life to fulfill the promise of American success. This dynamic is personified when Mrs. Woo is in a "stiff embraceless dance" with the television set (Tan). Hence, Mrs. Woo does not embrace the optimistic spirit of the American Dream, and instead considers it a necessary burden for her child. Consequently, Jing-mei recognizes that her mother's sacrifice is the foundation of Jing-mei's future aspirations. Moreover, this "dance" is only resolved when Mrs. Woo has her hand on the sound dial, carefully watching and controlling the television to make sure that *The Ed Sullivan Show* could be watched in its entirety. Thus, Mrs. Woo can only keep the American Dream alive if she has control of the narrative; without constant sacrifice and care, Mrs. Woo believes that Jing-mei would miss her opportunity at achieving American success.

The symbolism of the television as the American Dream becomes more direct as Tan reveals that the special guest on *The Ed Sullivan Show* is a nine-year-old Chinese girl, who masterfully plays the piano. Described as having a "Peter Pan haircut [...] [and] the sauciness of a Shirley Temple," Tan harkens toward the early moments of Jing-mei's childhood where she was characterized the same way (Tan). Through *The Ed Sullivan Show*, Mrs. Woo sees that Jing-mei's potential to achieve the American Dream was tangible. But while Jing-mei's mother focuses her attention on how the Chinese girl played the piano, Jing-mei fixates on the "fancy sweep of a curtsy" the girl did after her performance (Tan). Through the symbol of the curtsy, Jing-mei reveals that her intentions were not to achieve success in America in hopes of helping her and her mother out of poverty. Instead, Jing-mei craves the attention and validation that she never earned from her mother. Thus, the Chinese girl on television symbolizes two contrasting perspectives of the American Dream: while her mother sees the Chinese girl on television as what Jing-mei should strive to become, Jing-mei craves the praise and fame the girl received at the end of the performance.

While the television initially remains a symbol of optimism, the television ends up marking the death of the American Dream. When Mrs. Woo tells Jing-mei to turn off the television to attend piano lessons after her disastrous talent show performance, Jing-mei "planted herself more squarely" toward the television (Tan). For Mrs. Woo, the television now symbolizes a distraction for Jing-mei from the hard work needed to achieve American success. Contrastingly, the television remains a source of empowerment for Jing-mei: as Jing-mei embraces her individuality, the American Dream shifts from the burden of emulating the fame she saw in others to the freedom to explore what success means *for her*. Jing-mei even acknowledges that she felt as "if [her] true self had finally emerged" (Tan). This contrast of what the American Dream means is furthered when Mrs. Woo stands in front of the television, blocking Jing-mei's view. Hence, once Mrs. Woo realizes that Jing-mei would never be able to achieve her high expectations, Mrs. Woo's only goal is to have complete dominance over her daughter. And as Mrs. Woo physically drags her daughter away from the television, Jing-mei notes that she was "smiling crazily as if she were pleased that I was crying" (Tan). Amidst the shambles of the American Dream, Mrs. Woo would only be satisfied if her daughter would feel the pain of wasted sacrifices and empty dreams that she had felt. Thus, the painful reality of the American Dream is illustrated. For most who fail to achieve the success that is mythicized in immigrant families, the painful sacrifices both Jing-mei and her mother must make throughout their lives ends up destroying their lives.

Thus, within "Two Kinds," Amy Tan highlights the tragic illusion of the American Dream through the symbol of the television. Initially, the television represents how Jing-mei and her mother saw the American Dream. But as Jing-mei's aspirations for a bright future slowly begins to dim, she and her mother are forced to confront the reality of their pursuit for American success. For Jing-mei, the Dream becomes an empowering tool that rewards her for embracing her individuality. But for her mother, the Dream remains a constant reminder of the fruitless sacrifices she made for her daughter. By highlighting this conflict, Tan emphasizes the cost of the American Dream: when immigrant families place their hopes onto unattainable aspirations, the only pieces of wreckage left after being confronted with reality are the painful sacrifices made along the way.

Works Cited

Desowitz, Bill. "How Shirley Temple Got America to Stand up and Cheer." *USA Today*, Gannett Satellite Information Network, 12 Apr.2014. www.usatoday.com/story/life/books/2014/04/12/the-little-girl-who-fought-the-great-depression-shirley-temple-and-1930s-america/7515875/.

Tan, Amy. "Two Kinds." *The Joy Luck Club*. New York: Penguin, 2006. Print.

Honorable Mention—Humanities

Arthi Sivendra
Democracy: America's Greatest Scam

Two hundred and forty-four years ago, the United States was founded on the values of freedom and equality, but the freedom and equality of whom? The illustrious Founding Fathers, a group of rich white men, convened and decided their representation was of the utmost importance in civil society. As such, they needed to separate from Great Britain to ensure their rights. Thus, the wealthy American's version of democracy was born. Despite democracy appearing to be the bedrock of the American government, the United States is more accurately described as an oligarchy: a system where power is in the hands of an elite few. Instead of all voices being held equal, systems such as the Electoral College, privately funded campaigns, and restrictive voting practices limit the will of the people in favor of the rich.

In a country purporting that all voices are equal, the Electoral College is not only hypocritical but the antithesis of democracy. The reality of the situation is that "the electoral vote regularly deviates from the popular will as expressed in the popular vote... at times in such a way as to deny the presidency to the popular preference" (Edwards). Instead of considering the ballots of every voter, the Electoral College ignores the votes of anyone whose political affiliation does not line up with their state. Contrary to the American mythos, not every vote actually counts. In addition, this system effectively ensures that the voices of some are worth more than others through the creation of battleground states, destroying the notion of political equality. Under this system, "large states enjoy a theoretical advantage in being more likely than small states to cast the pivotal bloc of electoral votes in the electoral college... a large state is hypothetically more likely to be able to cast the vote that will determine the election" (Edwards). The way electoral votes are broken up causes candidates to focus more attention on large states instead of smaller states in hopes of pulling more votes. Therefore, there is a power discrepancy on the level of the individual voter and from state to state. When the position was created, the electors were meant "to be men of 'superior discernment, virtue and information' who would select the president 'according to their own will' and without reference to the immediate wishes of the people" (Edwards). If the point of representative democracy is for the people to choose officials to lead them, how does it make sense to have representatives from the Electoral College override their voice? These electors are often rich, led by their own biases, and not bound to vote in a way that aligns with their state's wishes. The Electoral College coddles the voter instead of honoring their choice. It demonstrates how the general lack of trust in the average American citizen spans the country's entire history. From its conception, the Electoral College puts the election in the hands of a few unchecked elite electors in a handful of states as opposed to the people.

In order to run a successful campaign to even be considered in the election, candidates rely on campaign donations that often come from the wealthy. Through empirical research, studies have found "that political campaign donations among elite are socially contagious. Being exposed to other donors increases chances of donation significantly" (Traag). From this, it follows that campaigns are primarily financed by the elite, which gives them an inordinate amount of power over the trajectory of a campaign. A substantial part of the reason a candidate is elected is because of the monetary support they receive from the wealthy, meaning they control who is voted into office. This influence does not end on the campaign trail, it carries over into their personal interests in policy. Due to a candidates' dependence on funding, some make the "argument that campaign contributions from interest groups may not represent quid pro quo bribery attempts by groups, but instead result from extortion by politicians who threaten to harm the groups' interests" (Gilens and Page 568). In exchange for money, candidates agree to not harm the interests of the wealthy. Moreover, research shows that these interests are not linked to the wants of the masses since the "net interest-group stands are not substantially correlated with the preferences of average citizens. Taking all interest groups together, the index of net interest-group alignment correlates only a non-significant .04 with average citizens' preferences" (Gilens and Page 570). This statistic puts campaigns into a whole new perspective. It is not about introducing the candidate to the people, but rather securing connections among the elite that only concern their own wants. Ultimately, money's prevalence in politics creates an institution built on shady backroom deals regarding the interests of the wealthy and politicians even if it stands against the will of the people.

    The main method Americans have for making their voice heard is voting, but even then, the United States has several systems in place to suppress the opinions of the people in favor of the rich. An overlooked aspect of passive voter suppression is how political parties approach, or avoid, potential voters. Political researchers "theorize about how this calculus of contact has led parties and campaigns to disproportionately ignore the poor in their political outreach," which is related to "the persistent rich–poor turnout gap" (Ross and Spencer 680). They disregard nonvoters which only continues the cycle of their lack of activity, thus contributing to their disenfranchisement. They use tactics such as microtargeting to avoid nonvoters which "led to increasing disparities in contact between higher and lower propensity voters" (Ross and Spencer 682). Many Americans when forced to choose between working or voting on a Tuesday will choose the one that feels more directly linked to their livelihood. Without the additional push from campaigns to vote, they are much less likely to feel as if their vote carries weight. As such, they will have to make the sacrifice the elite do not have to and work instead of vote. Therefore, depriving the electoral process of their opinion. It is fair to conclude that campaigns are not only funded by the rich but targeted at them as well. In every step of the equation, the voices of those who are not wealthy are seen as less important even by the people who are meant to represent them. They are not even significant enough to appeal to when on the campaign trail. This reaffirms the cycle of power of the rich in politics and government.

    Despite the flaws in American democracy, many believe it has benefits for the nation. They consider the current institution as a guarantee of a "freer world" that "directly benefits our own security, prosperity, and international standing" (Center for American Progress and Center for Strategic and International Studies 5). Comparisons are drawn between America and foreign tyrannical governments to highlight the positives of democracy, such as how it maintained stability in the nation. This conclusion came after having "examined 50 countries—both democratic and undemocratic—and [finding] overwhelming evidence that democracy supports development and reduces the likelihood of violent conflict" (Center for American Progress and Center for Strategic and International Studies 7). While the benefit of American democracy is giving people the ability to voice their discontent without risk of tyrannical punishment, it does not guarantee that the people will be heard. Stability simply means a structure set in its ways; in this case, it is the oligarchic institutions inherent in America. The American people should not be content with the way things are just because they could be worse. They must reflect on the power imbalances within the government and work to rectify them to create a more equal institution. The first step to doing so is utilizing the popular vote and taking money out of politics. Both measures take away the influence of the rich and equally distribute it among the people. When compared to some foreign nations, American democracy may be the better alternative, but that does not mean the nation should shy away from critical reflection of its own faults. This analysis is the only path to a solution.

From its origins, as much as the United States has prided itself on democracy, it has always fallen short. At every given opportunity from campaigning to voting to enacting public policy, the voice of the people is always second to the rich. The elite have managed to have a monopoly over the government. In terms of voting, the votes of the collective people are less important than those of several select electors. Also, the poorer voter is often overlooked by campaigns in favor of those who have more money. Beyond voting, the wealthy control the success of campaigns through donations. This gives them influence over public policy when compared to the average American. Fundamentally, America was never a country of the people, it was always an oligarchy committed to advancing the wants of the economic elite. As such, it is in the hands of the people to fight for change in this corrupt system.

Works Cited

Center for American Progress, and Center for Strategic and International Studies. "Why Promoting Democracy Is Smart and Right." Center for American Progress, 2013. https://www.americanprogress.org/wp-content/uploads/2013/01/StatementofPrinciples-2.pdf. Accessed 29 Oct. 2020.

Edwards, George C. *Why the Electoral College Is Bad for America*, 2nd edition. Yale University Press, 2011.

Gilens, Martin and Benjamin I. Page. "Testing Theories of American Politics: Elites, Interest Groups, and Average Citizens." *Perspectives on Politics,* vol. 12, no. 03, 14 Sept. 2014, pp.564-581,scholar.princeton.edu/sites/default/files/mgilens/files/gilens_and_page_2014_-testing_theories_of_american_politics.doc.pdf, 10.1017/s1537592714001595. Accessed 29 Oct. 2020.

Ross, Bertrall L., and Douglas M. Spencer. "Passive Voter Suppression: Campaign Mobilization and the Effective Disfranchisement of the Poor." *Northwestern University Law Review*, vol. 114, no. 03, 20 Nov. 2019, papers.ssrn.com/sol3/papers.cfm?abstract_id=3501739. Accessed 29 Oct. 2020.

Traag, Vincent A. "Complex Contagion of Campaign Donations." *PloS One*, vol. 11, no. 4, Public Library of Science (PLoS), Apr. 2016, pp. e0153539 e0153539, doi:10.1371/journal.pone.0153539.

First Place—Social Sciences

Hope Wilson
Gender Roles and the Continued Imperialism of America

As sexuality and gender have become hot debate topics in recent years, the push for transgender rights has been moved to the forefront. The simple act of using a public restroom presents many within the LGBTQ+ community with a difficult choice, exposing them to an onslaught of verbal attacks no matter what they choose. As Arnold Grossman, professor of applied psychology at New York University, puts it, "exhibiting gender-atypical behavior makes transgender youth an especially vulnerable population" (113). Looking back on U.S. history, the problem with gender expression acceptance isn't just the ignorant minds of today, but those of our ancestors, creating a culture of imperialistic nature.

History is taught by the winners, especially with the United States' teachings of native cultures. Despite different Native American societies acknowledging three to five genders, society today tells us there are only two. Duane Brayboy, member of the Tosneoc Tuscarora Community, says the term varied from tribe to tribe, but the universal English term for transgender Native Americans is "Two Spirit." Brayboy then describes Two Spirit people as often "highly revered," considered lucky, fearless, had high functioning intellect, and held respectable positions in the tribes, such as keepers of oral tradition. In the tradition of Two Spirit, "Native Americans traditionally assign no moral gradient in love or sexuality; a person was judged for their contributions to their tribe and for their character." In some tribes, children lived among gender-neutral roles until they decided for themselves which path to follow. Brayboy continues to detail how after exposure to this aspect of Native culture, colonizers returned to their respective countries with fears, as seen in George Catlin's claims that the Two Spirit tradition "must be extinguished before it can be more fully recorded." This European prejudice would expand to later Euro-Americans, demanding conformity to their two genders throughout the United States' history, with claims "that there were no alternative genders among the Six Nations Iroquois/Haudenosaunee, despite documentation and oral histories," continuing lasting Eurocentric ideals (Brayboy par. 1-8). Dean Spade, associate professor of law at Seattle University, describes how "imperialism and militarism" have erased Native American gender concepts by using "sexual, gender, and family norms as technologies of intervention and violence" (7). Imperialism has directly wiped out Native American culture, especially the concepts of gender and sexual identity.

Despite modern knowledge of the Native tradition of Two Spirit and gender dysphoria, the United States still follows the tradition of binary genders, with forced compliance leaving detrimental effects on transgender people today. It is particularly harmful to the transgender youth, as they try to discover who they are, defying expectations that society has forced them to swallow. Grossman analyzes a study exploring the experiences of transgender youth (ages 15 to 21), revealing four health-related vulnerabilities: "the lack of safe environments, poor access to physical health services, inadequate resources to address their mental health concerns, and a lack of continuity of caregiving by their families and communities." These problems all stem from the fact that transgender existence defies the traditional status quo. According to Grossman, it is difficult to feel seen when "individuals are expected to assume the gender of their biological sex as well as the gender expectations and roles associated with it." Additionally, transgender youth are seen as especially vulnerable "to a lack of resources and increased risk associated with discrimination, marginalization and disenfranchisement." These harmful outcomes have direct negative effects to the mental health of transgender youth, as their true self often must remain hidden. Without proper access to the help they need, Grossman explains that many resort to self-harm, or other unhealthy coping mechanisms. Being forced to distance themselves from religious parents, or staying and bearing physical and mental abuse, prompts trauma that can last for a lifetime. Finally, life at school can further deteriorate mental health, as "with the lack of support at home and the routine stigmatization at school, many had experienced serious academic difficulties and dropped out of school" (Grossman 7-14). Living in a world created around the gender binary confines transgender youth into a box that is ultimately harmful to their well-being.

This problem is best solved through the education of closed-minded people, however, there are more logistical steps that can be taken. Organizations such as the Trevor Project exist to help suicide prevention in LGBTQ+ youth, and additional organizations will certainly help mental health. The more support available, especially if it can be accessed without parental consent or knowledge, is crucial to creating a better situation for transgender youth. As discussed previously, the abuse faced from parents that don't accept their gender or sexual expression is particularly harmful as it is a strained relationship, but is also oftentimes a blockade standing between the individual and the help they need. Emilia Lombardi, associate professor in public health at Baldwin Wallace University, says it's important to "advocate for cultural relevancy within research, policy, education and prevention programs," as well as increase health care, such as "public and private third-party coverage of hormones and surgeries needed for people to change their legal sex, greater input of transgender individuals in their own care, and more education on transgender health care issues" (3). In addition, implementing education on Two-Spirit into schools across the country will introduce kids to the topic, so they feel more accepting towards gender and sexuality exploration. With education and advocacy, the world can truly become a better place and become more embracing of transgender individuals.

The fight for equal rights and representation for transgender individuals is one that everyone should be a part of. Starting proper education for kids all across the United States on Two Spirit would lead to increased awareness and acceptance towards gender-queer people. The imperialistic nature by which the United States was formed and operates has tried to erase an entire sea of cultures, and it is our duty to make sure they are not lost forever.

Works Cited

Brayboy, Duane. "Two Spirits, One Heart, Five Genders." *IndianCountryToday.com*, Indian Country

Today, 7 Sept. 2017, indiancountrytoday.com/archive/two-spirits-one-heart-five-genders-9UH_xnbfVEWQHWkjNn0rQQ.

Grossman, Arnold H., and Anthony R. D'augelli. "Transgender Youth." *Journal of Homosexuality*, vol. 51, no. 1, 2006, pp. 111–128., doi:10.1300/j082v51n01_06.

Lombardi, E. "Enhancing transgender health care." *American Journal of Public Health* vol. 91,6 (2001): 869-72. doi:10.2105/ajph.91.6.869

Spade, Dean, and Craig Willse. "Sex, Gender, and War in an Age of Multicultural Imperialism." *QED: A Journal in GLBTQ Worldmaking*, vol. 1, no. 1, 2014, pp. 5–29. JSTOR, www.jstor.org/stable/10.14321/qed.1.1.0005. Accessed 5 Oct. 2020.

Second Place—Social Sciences

Sky Harper
Shidine'e doo Shidziil (My People, My Strength)

More than 2,000 miles away, the ties between my family and I have been drawn taut, yet remain unsevered. For the past 19 years these ties have been reinforced and strengthened. Each is wound tightly to form an intricate and durable braid, strong enough to support any strain. I never paid much attention to how intricate my family is, yet as I reflect on my early life, I am astonished and appreciative for the family that I grew to know. In the lives of the Navajo, family plays a vital role in day-to-day interactions and is embedded deep within our founding philosophies. Our families are not solely based on blood, but also kinship. For us however, kinship has evolved into a much more elaborate and intimate entity known as clanship. In the Four Corners region of the United States, clanship relations between individuals are one aspect beneath the umbrella known as "K'e."

There are many teachings and philosophies associated with K'e that aim to support individuals as they develop and mature. From my family, I learned that K'e is parallel to health. An individual, regardless of age or background, cannot be considered healthy emotionally, spiritually, mentally, nor physically—if they lack a stable family network or support system. According to Gary Witherspoon, a non-Navajo scientist who aimed to study K'e, "kinship as a system is a set of concepts, beliefs, and attitudes about solidarity. The solidarity governed by kinship is generally more intense, more diffuse, and more enduring than other kinds of solidarity"(12-13). I completely agree with Witherspoon's observation that kinship/K'e produces a much more intense solidarity than relationships that are not governed by K'e, such as friendships.

The Navajo are one of the most studied indigenous cultures in the world; however, their social organization is one of the least understood (12-13). As a Navajo youth, even though I grew up constantly exposed to K'e and the teachings associated with it, there are still many elements that I struggle to fully grasp. I can only imagine how overwhelmed and lost an outsider would be when looking into our culture. However, through his research, Witherspoon hoped to gain fundamental insight on how the social structure functioned and how it played a role in the development of individuals throughout their lives. Most notable, Witherspoon observed that the Navajo demonstrated a matriarchal society where the females were the central foundation of the family. Being a matriarchal society, the Navajos practiced and displayed a more peaceful lifestyle than neighboring tribes. They lived a nomadic life, following livestock and water, before eventually transitioning to an agricultural lifestyle, and ending their peripatetic ways. The development of agricultural practices depended greatly on the efforts of the entire family. Every member was given responsibilities and was trusted to carry them out to the best of their ability. There was an overall emphasis on peace and respect rather than warring parties and raids.

Much like my ancestors, spending time with my family was a central part of my life. During the winter, I used to spend the days and nights indoors, shielded from the snow and cold. I would sit near the fireplace while my grandparents told me stories. Eventually, the rest of my family would gather and listen to the creation of the world or stories of our ancestors. My grandfather would tell me that there were four main clans that were created directly from the body of the deity, Changing Woman. These four clans became her children, whom she loved and cherished with all her heart. From Changing Woman, the first Navajos learned the teachings associated with K'e. These teachings were based on the home and family. An individual's first clan, the clan they self-identify with, came from their mother. Their second clan comes from their father, their third from their maternal grandfather, and fourth from their paternal grandfather. The model for the Navajo concept regarding relationships is based on the relationship that Changing Woman had cultured with the universe and her children (Manuelito). My grandparents and parents would tell me how Changing Woman treated every living and nonliving entity with respect, for everything had a spirit, animate or not. She made sure to appreciate and give thanks, from the sunlight to the smallest drops of rain. Changing Woman established that in this world we are never alone. If there is a breeze, water, or sunlight, your ancestors and spirits will always be around to guide you. From these stories, I learned that I am never truly alone. I also learned to look at the positive and be thankful for what I have, instead of focusing on what I do not have. In this way, my mental, emotional, and spiritual health have benefited. I learned to be thankful, rather than being jealous or envious.

Along with developing our sense of community in the universe, the teaching of K'e has also taught us how to interact with one another. These interactions are guided by clanship. There may be one or more groups of the same clan living great distances away from each other. However, each clan group establishes a strong sense of family. If an individual found themselves in need of help, the community would unite to lend a hand. If an individual found themselves in another area that may have the same clan, a new network is established and can be kindled to become more intimate.

I am Dzilth Nee T'ah Kinyaa'aanii (Near the Mountain—Towering House clan), born for Tachiinii (Red Running into Water clan). My maternal grandfather is Tohtsoni (Big Water clan), and my paternal grandfather is Kinyaa'aanii (Towering House clan). Each of my clans are a part of who I am. I grew up hearing stories of how our clans came to be and what responsibilities Changing Woman had bestowed upon us. I grew up, knowing that my actions carried weight. I could do my best to represent my family or I could make the wrong decisions and soil my family's name. However, I also learned that when I faced a challenge, I would always have people who I could lean on for support.

The way the clan system functions is very sophisticated. If someone had at least one of the same four clans as another individual, the two would be considered relatives. If I met an individual whose mother was Dzilth Nee T'ah Kinyaa'aanii, I would greet them as my brother or sister—if they were in the same age group as me. However, if they were older, I would greet them as my mother, uncle, or grandmother/grandfather. Ultimately, these clan-family connections aid individuals while also assigning various obligations onto others, so that as mentioned before, a bigger, more diffuse, tight-knit community is created.

The elders who identify as grandfathers oversee storytelling and traditions in the family. The grandfather ensures that traditions stay alive and are honored. Uncles oversee scolding and the discipline of children when necessary. Fathers are the providers who work to keep the family safe and secure. Mothers and maternal grandmothers are the caretakers and glue that hold the family together and ensure that the spirit of the home is nurtured. Meanwhile, paternal grandmothers and paternal aunts hold different roles within the family. As children grow and develop with exposure to K'e and clanship, they are assigned various roles in the family. Some children fulfill the roles of an uncle or mother figure because of their clan-connection with others. In this way, children mature faster and learn self-awareness, establishing their place in the family and in the universe. A few of the connections I have are with many male elders. I refer to them as Cheii (grandpa), and they refer to me as "Cheii yazhi" (little grandpa). With many elders, I do my best to help them when I can, splitting wood or feeding livestock. In return, they share their stories and wisdom with me. Growing up with this lifestyle and sense of responsibility, became a self-aware individual.

Evident throughout the essay, Navajo communities are not comparable to the definition of a euro-western community. Navajo communities may extend hundreds of miles throughout the Navajo Nation and even further, depending on where individuals reside. For instance, I moved to Philadelphia to attend Drexel University, two thousand miles away from my family. However, I learned that I have a grandfather who lives two hours north of Philly who is related to me through clan. I have been able to create and strengthen a relationship that did not previously exist. I have found a new support system to help guide me through the unfamiliar territory. Furthermore, I find myself to be self-motivated and disciplined, knowing that I represent my entire family and clan. If I were to stumble or find myself on the wrong path in life, my actions would reflect on them.

In my experience, K'e has been vital throughout my life. My family taught me to acknowledge relatives through my clans. Through these connections, I became more open minded, and surrounded by family who care deeply for me, and whom I can always lean on for support. My definition of family is different from many other people's definition, yet it has strengthened me. From sitting at the fireplace with my family, to listening to stories, or lending a hand to someone who needs help, my family has molded me into the person I am today. I know that I am never truly alone, and when I feel homesick, I look outside at the clouds and take a drink of water, acknowledging the spirits around me. *Hozho naashaa doo... With beauty before me, I walk.*

Works Cited

Manuelito, Kathryn D. A Dine (Navajo) "Perspective on Self-Determination: An Exposition of an Egalitarian Place." *Taboo, Spring-Summer 2006.*

Witherspoon, Gary. *Navajo Kinship and Marriage.* Chicago: The University of Chicago Press, 1975. Book.

Honorable Mention—Social Sciences

Ellie DiPaolo
The Impact of Teacher Efficacy on Student Performance

Any child enrolled in public school since the wide-spread installation of the active board has probably been stuck in a class with a lesson plan that mostly consisted of a constant loop of YouTube videos. A portion of my high school classes were spent like this too. Unfortunately, ineffective teachers that lack a passion for their subject often result in a classroom of unmotivated students, me included. My best teachers, with their great dedication to education, inspired their students to try, despite the subject matter. The effort that teachers put forth to motivate their students is called teacher efficacy. My experience in classes I loved and loathed in high school has convinced me that teacher efficacy has a positive impact on student performance.

There is much more to understand on the subject of teacher efficacy. Generally, teacher efficacy is a measure of a "teacher's sense of competence-not some objective measure of actual competence," meaning their capabilities in the classroom are more important than a particularly high IQ (Protheroe). A teacher's proficiency in the classroom can also be linked to several key characteristics such as increased preparation and organization, receptivity to criticism and new learning methods, resilience, and coping with arduous students. These practices result in a deeper connection to their subject material and the students they are teaching. When reflecting on the traits of my own high school teachers, I found that this was an accurate measure of their own proficiency. My teachers that relied heavily on busywork and constantly changed the class calendar, while also becoming combative when students told them they were struggling, were not effective teachers. Several of my AP classes with these teaching styles would see their sizes cut in half within the first few weeks of the school year due to students dropping to a lower-level class. However, my teachers that relied on strict regimens for their lessons, but also took the time to go back and re-teach material my classmates and I missed on quizzes and tests, would be considered educators with greater efficacy. I often scored much higher in those subjects as a result of my teachers' commitment to education.

The umbrella term of teacher efficacy has also been divided into two smaller subsets by researchers: personal and general teaching efficacy. "Personal teaching efficacy relates to a teacher's own feeling of confidence in regard to teaching abilities" while general teaching efficacy refers to the belief that teaching has the ability to impact students (Protheroe). Thus, these two ideas are independent from one another because a teacher can lack confidence in their own ability, while still believing in the power of education. Mastery of both elements of teacher efficacy can happen during a teacher's first years of teaching, resulting from the belief that they are making an impact on the lives of their students. Efficacy can also develop from other teachers and the overall environment of the school. This concept refers to collective teacher efficacy, and is seen in schools where teachers are encouraged to work together and there exists a general belief that students can be taught despite hardships such as poverty or limited knowledge of English. A study conducted in 2002 determined that collective efficacy "was more important in explaining school achievement than socioeconomic status," proving that teachers have a profound impact on the success of their students (Protheroe). Collective efficacy is often set by the leadership of the school and the guidance of the principal. A principal who values continuing teacher education, shared lesson plans, and a welcoming environment encourages collective efficacy in the school.

Increased student performance due to teacher efficacy has been the subject of numerous studies beginning in the 1980s. A meta-analysis conducted by Robert M. Klassen examined 43 of these studies, all published between 1985 and 2003, included 9,216 teacher participants in total. The author included studies that measured "teachers' psychological characteristics labeled as self-efficacy or personality" to find the link between teaching efficacy and student performance (Klassen). Researchers found that teachers who were able to maintain desirable psychological characteristics in the classroom such as emotional stability and stress tolerance had a positive impact on their students. "Teachers are emotional contagions" resulting in both positive and negative emotions being passed directly onto their students (Klassen). Through this meta-analysis, Klassen found a positive statistical association ($r=.08$, $p<.05$) between teacher personality and effectiveness. Confirming that a teacher with effective traits has a more positive impact on their classroom in comparison to teachers with inadequate beliefs about their own skills in the classroom.

One of my favorite classes of my senior year was AP Statistics. This was not because I love math, it is actually one of my least favorite subjects, but my teacher was incredibly positive. He taught using very creative lesson plans and always took the mood of his students into consideration. If someone came to class visibly upset, he let them take the quiz or test another day. This uplifting emotional environment had a great impact on me and I looked forward to attending Statistics every day. Thus, my grades for math my senior year were the highest I achieved since middle school. If more students were exposed to effective teachers dedicated to positive learning styles, they would mostly likely see an increase in performance as well.

A more recent study called "Does motivation matter?—The relationship between teachers' self-efficacy and enthusiasm and students' performance" conducted in 2018 measured the performance of 1,036 biology students at the beginning and end of a unit about the ecosystem of the Wadden Sea to examine the impacts of teacher efficacy. Through a careful study of informative questionnaires completed by the students' 48 teachers, researchers Daniela Maler, Jorg Groszschedl, and Ute Harms found a link between student performance and teacher efficacy after a thorough statistical analysis. They used data models to identify a positive trend in the work ethic of students participating in the study, which could be applied to teacher-student relationships beyond this analysis. The study concluded that "successful teaching requires more than professional knowledge, by revealing a positive relationship between teacher enthusiasm and students' performance," reaffirming the belief that teacher efficacy is not about individual intelligence, but a desire to motivate children (Mahler).

There is even evidence that teacher efficacy impacts students beyond academic performance. Scientists have found that as our brains grow and develop during adolescence, they require safety and warmth (Terada). Thus, the brain has been found to learn more effectively in positive environments than negative ones. This means that schools practicing collective teacher efficacy are more likely to experience higher attendance rates, test scores, and graduation rates. Researcher C. Kirabo Jackson examined the data for over 570,000 ninth-grade students in North Carolina and found that "teachers who improved their students' noncognitive skills" experienced similar impacts (Terada). In addition, Jackson also found that these students were less likely to be suspended or held back a grade. When a positive environment is created for learning, student cognitive skills are improved in addition to academic grades. Skills like self-regulation and motivation result in life skills that last beyond school. In comparison to other aspects of schooling, "teachers have the greatest impact on student achievement" due to how they affect their students as people in addition to academics (Terada).

Teachers are the backbone of the American education system; they not only impact students numerically through test scores, but also instill in them the desire to learn and succeed. My best teachers were some of my biggest supporters, advocates, and inspirations. Hiring teachers that possess the efficacy to mold the minds of our next generation is important. Developing collective teacher efficacy in schools is essential to ensure that teachers are supported by a community that they can learn from as well. In a time where the United States is falling behind in the education level of its children, prioritizing effective teachers is necessary to improve the performance of its youngest citizens.

Works Cited

Klassen, Robert M. "Teachers' Self-Efficacy, Personality, and Teaching Effectiveness: A Meta-Analysis."*Educational Research Review*, vol. 12, 2014, pp. 59–79, doi:10.15417/1881.

Mahler, Daniela, et al. "Does motivation matter?—The relationship between teachers' self-efficacy and enthusiasm and students' performance."*PLoS ONE*, vol. 13, no. 11, 2018, p. e0207352. *Gale AcademicOneFile*,https://link.gale.com/apps/doc/ Accessed 24 Oct. 2020.

Protheroe, Nancy. Principal, 2008, pp. 42–45,*Teacher Efficacy: What Is It and Does It Matter?*

Terada, Youki. "Understanding a Teacher's Long-Term Impact." *Edutopia*, George Lucas Educational Foundation, 4 Feb. 2019, www.edutopia.org/article/understanding-teachers-long-term-impact.

Honorable Mention—Social Sciences

Samuel Weinstein
The Gravity of Personality

Throughout a student's career, they are taught by an array of different teachers, all of whom are unique individuals with varying personalities. When you hear the phrase "good teacher," what kind of person do you imagine? Do you imagine someone with a vibrant and colorful personality that inspires hard work and passion amongst their students? Or do you imagine someone with a dull personality that encourages laziness and apathy amongst their students? Most likely, you imagine a person resembling the former. While this might seem like *prima facie* speculation, the notion that there are "good" teachers, as well as "bad" ones, is a truthful one. But what defines a "good" teacher? And what makes a teacher "bad?" Something "good" creates a desirable outcome by the constructed social standards of a specific culture. Therefore, high-achieving students, driven by a positive attitude toward learning, can be considered a desirable outcome by social standards of Western culture. Thus, a "good" teacher is capable of producing high achieving students with positive attitudes toward learning and, a "bad" teacher is incapable of producing such an outcome.

My teachers' personalities have always had a significant impact on my attitude toward the subject they were teaching. If I *did not* like my teacher's personality, I was prone to slacking off and underperforming. However, if I *did* like my teacher's personality, I was uber interested in learning the material and motivated to do all the work to the best of my ability. In general, I found it a lot easier to enjoy learning when the person teaching me was enjoyable themself. In my experience, when you enjoy doing something, success typically follows. My teachers that taught with visible passion, expressed care for their students, and always kept an open ear for constructive criticism, never failed to make learning in their classroom enjoyable. Consequently, they made success an attainable venture with little struggles along the way.

According to a 2019 study in the *Educational Psychology Review*, there is a specific combination of characteristics or qualities that form a good teacher. These characteristics are defined by the Big Five personality domains: openness, conscientiousness, extraversion, agreeableness, and emotional stability (Kim et al.). Openness is a quality that reflects one's ability to be flexible and engage with new ideas and opinions (Kim et al.). Conscientiousness entails the ability to be achievement-focused, highly responsible, and organized (Kim et al.). Extraversion is associated with high levels of assertive communication, social sensitivity, and disclosure (Kim et al.). Agreeableness is a strong indicator of empathy, warmness, and kindness (Kim et al.). Lastly, emotional stability denotes the ability to consistently remain level-headed, secure, and stress-free (Kim et al.). The results of the *Educational Psychology* Review study suggest that a teacher whose behavior frequently displays all the aforementioned personality traits positively correlates with teacher effectiveness as measured by student academic achievement.

In my experience as a student, having a teacher that displays even one of the five Big Five personality domains has allowed me to be more successful for a multitude of reasons. With respect to openness, if I had a teacher that wanted to hear suggestions about the direction of their instruction or the criteria for a new assignment, it made their class feel refreshing and engaging. Allowing students to give their input also communicates a level of respect that the teacher has for their students by empowering the students to voice their opinions. A student's ability to have control over the direction of their learning can be motivating and lead to more student success, but this all comes as a result of the teacher exhibiting openness (Wood). Concerning conscientiousness, a teacher that is highly organized and lays out well-defined goals for the class provides their students with direction, resulting in a clearer path to success (Meador). Whenever I had a teacher who made the purpose of their instruction clear, success in their class always felt very realistic. When it comes to extraversion, having a sociable teacher that frequently engaged with me during class made me feel appreciated and, as a result, more comfortable in the classroom. Extraversion in tandem with agreeableness creates a dynamic that promotes casual, open communication between the teacher and the students, which makes students more willing to seek help when they need it, allowing them to be as academically successful as possible (Stenger). Finally, with emotional stability, teachers that demonstrate a consistent mood provide their students with a consistent learning environment where they know what to expect in each class. After having both emotionally stable and emotionally sporadic teachers, I can say with great certainty that it was much easier for me to achieve the grades I wanted when I knew what to expect from my teacher's behavior going into each class.

A teacher that does not possess any of the traits defined by the Big Five personality domains is probably not going to be a good one. So, what components of a teacher's personality make them ineffective or "bad?" According to a 2019 study in the *Global Journal of Human-Social Science*, three main "negative teaching characteristics" deem a teacher ineffective or "bad." Namely, impatience, quickness to anger, and rigidity (Maazouzi). These are all characteristics of a teacher that creates apathy amongst their students. Impatience leads to rushing through important topics during class and unclear explanations of how to do complex assignments (Maazouzi). A teacher that regularly displays impatience causes their students to hold themselves to lower expectations due to the lack of clarity in the teacher's instruction (Maazouzi). Impatience is often indicative of a short temper, also known as quickness to anger (Maazouzi). Whenever I had a teacher that was prone to having emotional explosions over silly mistakes, I was significantly less likely to approach them or seek any form of help from them. This typically resulted in me struggling more frequently and settling for lower grades. A teacher that is quick to anger automatically undermines their students' trust and respect and fails to be positively influential (Maazouzi). Furthermore, quickness to anger is naturally born out of rigidity. Teachers that project rigidity tend to embody inflexibility and lack openness to suggestions from students (Maazouzi). For me, having a teacher who blatantly displayed rigidity on a regular basis made me considerably less inclined to communicate with them and vastly more uncomfortable simply sitting in their class. In general, rigidity can harm students by inhibiting their ability to learn, thus inhibiting their ability to be as academically successful as possible (Maazouzi). A "bad" teacher embodies any or all of the three "negative teaching characteristics" defined by the *Global Journal of Human-Social Science*.

When examining the fundamental components of a "good" teacher's personality it's important to keep in mind that no one is perfect. There is not a single teacher who completely embodies every single trait defined by the Big Five personality domains. However, a "good" teacher must embody at least one of the five Big Five personality domains to impact their students positively. Not only that, but a truly "good" teacher must not consistently take part in any behavior that exhibits impatience, quickness to anger, or rigidity, all of which are characteristics that promote student apathy, suppress open communication, and inhibit high academic achievement. A truly "good" teacher is flexible in their instruction, allowing students to have some control over what they learn and how they learn it. A truly "good" teacher makes the goals of their instruction clear and attainable, while actively attempting to create an open inquisitive dialogue with their students, as well as a consistent and, therefore, low-stress learning environment. A teacher whose personality enables this behavior holds the key to effective teaching and high academic achievement among students.

Works Cited

Kim, Lisa E., et al. "A Meta-Analysis of the Effects of Teacher Personality on Teacher Effectiveness and Burnout." *Educational Psychology Review*, vol. 31, no. 1, Springer Science and Business Media LLC, Jan. 2019, pp. 163–95.

Maazouzi, Karima. "The Impact of Teacher's Personality and Behavior on Students' Achievement." *Global Journal of Human-Social Science*, vol. 19, no. 9, ser. 1.0, 2019, pp. 25–30.

Meador, Derrick "Do You Have the Traits to Be a Successful Teacher or Student?" *ThoughtCo, Dotdash*, 5 July 2019.

Stenger, Marianne "10 Reasons Why Extroverted Teachers Rock the Education World." *Whooo's Reading Blog*, 20 June 2017.

Wood, Zachary R. "The Benefits of Intellectual Open-Mindedness." *Times Higher Education (THE)*, 18 Dec. 2015.

The Zelda Provenzano Endowed STEM Writing Award

Vivek Babu

The Hygiene Hypothesis, Microbial "Old Friends," and the COVID-19 Pandemic

During the COVID-19 pandemic, as many have become resistant to strict lockdown measures, some individuals suggest that using hand sanitizer and wearing masks too often could weaken our immune system. This "hygiene hypothesis," first proposed in 1989 by British immunologist David P. Strachan, has remained enshrined in popular culture, "We're too clean for our own good" (Apostolopoulos et al., 2020). A survey conducted by the Royal Society for Public Health in June 2019 found that almost one in four (23%) individuals agreed with the statement that "hygiene in the home is not important because children need to be exposed to harmful germs to build their immune system" (Royal Society for Public Health, 2019). With the majority of media propagating this "Hygiene Hypothesis" to the public, dangerous misconceptions about the role of personal hygiene in the development of allergies and autoimmune disorders have played a detrimental role in protecting children's immune systems (Scudellari, 2017). Thus, this paper aims to gain a broader understanding of how the "Hygiene Hypothesis" has been disproven, while understanding the merits of other immunological theories, namely the more accepted "Old Friends" hypothesis.

History and Evolution of the Hygiene Hypothesis

One of the first observations about how infectious pathogens contribute to immune dysregulation was B.M. Greenwood's finding in 1969 that Western Nigeria had a low incidence of rheumatoid arthritis. He theorized that frequent exposure to malaria might contribute to this disparity (Stiemsma et al., 2015). A year later, Greenwood further supported this theory by observing suppressed spontaneous autoimmune disease in mice infected with Plasmodium Berghei, which causes rodent malaria (Stiemsma et al., 2015). In 1976, Gerrard et al. found this same disparity between rural and urbanized communities by finding a decreased rate of allergies in indigenous populations in Northern Canada compared to urban Caucasian populations (Stiemsma et al., 2015).

The origins of the classic Hygiene Hypothesis can be traced to David P. Strachan's 1989 paper, "Hay fever, hygiene, and household size" in the British Medical Journal. Strachan substantiated this theory in 1996 by examining family history, medical records, and allergy skin prick test results in 11,765 children and finding that household size was inversely correlated with the development of hay fever (Stiemsma et al., 2015). He hypothesized that this trend arose because children can be exposed to germs by older siblings, developing a degree of immunity to hay fever. In contrast, a lack of early childhood exposure to unhygienic conditions can increase an individual's susceptibility to allergies (Strachan, 1989).

Strachan's hypothesis was later expanded upon by Dr. Erika von Mutius in the late 1990s. Mutius' study centered on comparing the rates of allergies and asthma in children who grew up in former East and West Germany. Mutius' initial hypothesis was that East German children, who grew up in less hygienic and poorer environmental conditions (heavy air pollution, for example) would exhibit incidences of allergies and asthma greater than their Western counterparts (Mutius, 2006). However, her research found the opposite: children in the polluted areas of East Germany had lower allergic reactions and fewer cases of asthma than children in West Germany. Mutius' work suggested that children who are around numerous other children or animals early in life are exposed to more microbes, and their immune systems develop more tolerance for the antigens that cause asthma (Mutius, 2010).

However, Strachan's observations about the epidemiological disparities in allergic diseases did not have an immunological backing, until Dr. Tim Mosmann and Dr. Robert Coffman's findings about the T-helper 1 (Th1) and T-helper 2 (Th2) cell subtypes. Mosmann and Coffman found that T-cells in mice secreted two separate cytokine profiles: the proinflammatory Th1 state and the anti-inflammatory Th2 state (Stiemsma et al., 2015). Th2 cells play a primary role in the allergen sensitization process. Infection with viruses and intracellular bacteria stimulates Th1 immune responses, which suppress Th2 cytokine activity through proinflammatory cytokines (Stiemsma et al., 2015).

Currently, while the "Hygiene Hypothesis" has branched to encompass dozens of related variables including environmental pressure, medication, diet, parasite infection, and others, many researchers have questioned its limiting factors (Alexandre-Silva, 2018). As more research attempts to connect the link between hygiene and microbial exposure, the "Hygiene Hypothesis" is revealed to be increasingly inaccurate. To date, there is no confirmed evidence of the link between personal/home cleanliness and increased risk of allergic disease. Moreover, microbial studies in westernized homes indicate that daily or weekly cleaning habits (even with antibacterial cleaners) have no sustained effect on the levels of microbes in the home (Bloomfield, 2019). Immunologist Sally Bloomfield further notes that Rook's understanding of excess cleanliness is implausible because of how fast microbes can spread, even after their removal. Thus, this criticism of Strachan's "Hygiene Hypothesis," has ushered in the widespread acceptance of Rook's 2003 "Old Friends" hypothesis, which observes immune dysregulation through an evolutionary lens.

Mechanisms and Current Understanding of the "Old Friends" Hypothesis

Proposed as an alternative to David Strachan's "Hygiene Hypothesis," Graham Rook's "Old Friends" hypothesis argues that the vital microbial exposures needed to train the immune system are not the childhood infections that Strachan theorized a decade prior (Bloomfield et al., 2016). Instead, Rook approached pathogen exposure through the lens of evolutionary medicine. The "Old Friends" hypothesis argues that certain microbes co-evolved with humans during primate evolution and in hunter-gatherer societies (Cepon-Robins & Gildner, 2020). Since these microbes had to be tolerated, the immune system responded by developing strategies to activate certain immunoregulatory mechanisms (Alexandre-Silva, 2018). Furthermore, Rook's hypothesis argues that living with personal "anti-hygienic" habits does not correlate with higher incidences of chronic inflammatory and allergic diseases (Bloomfield et al., 2016). Rook justifies this theory by characterizing most common childhood infections (such as smallpox, tuberculosis, and the flu) as "crowd infections" because they only flourish in large, crowded communities. Rook furthers that because these "crowd infections" came too late into the evolution of the immune system, exposure to these dangerous infectious pathogens is nonessential to building a strong immune system. Instead, the "Old Friends" hypothesis states that early exposure to a specific group of antigens present during human's early evolution (also known as "old friends") is essential for the immune system to properly respond to novel microbes (Bloomfield et al., 2016).

The "Old Friends" hypothesis further attempts to understand the disproportional rise of allergies and autoimmune diseases in wealthy, urbanized nations as compared to low-income nations. Rook explains that the advancement of medical, hygiene, and sanitation practices has limited the exposure to these "old friends." This lack of microbial exposure results in immune dysregulation that favors pro-inflammatory pathways, which overreact to benign microorganisms (Cepon-Robins & Gildner, 2020). Thus, the "Old Friends" hypothesis marks a clear paradigm shift for understanding the correlation between urbanization and wealth and weakened immune system from a lack of microbes in general toward the lack of exposure to specific "old friends," known as evolutionary mismatch.

The core argument behind Rook's "Old Friends" hypothesis is that "old friends" exposure at a young age is critical to developing a functional immune system. That said, only certain types of "old friends" co-evolved with human immune systems. The "old friends" include commensal bacteria, which reside on the skin, gut, and respiratory tract; environmental microbiota through air, soil, and water; and helminths, which are parasitic worms that have mutualistically co-evolved with humans in order to survive (Alexandre-Silva, 2018). Beyond the microorganisms, "old infections" (such as variations of *Mycobacterium tuberculosis*) were also critical to the evolving immune system because they were found in persistent non-fatal carrier states within small isolated hunter-gatherer groups (Rook et al., 2014). This is perhaps where Strachan's "Hygiene Hypothesis" most sharply differed from Rook's "Old Friends Hypothesis." Strachan argued that exposure to conventional childhood infections, such as measles, chickenpox, and mumps was needed to train the immune system. Rook argued that these "crowd infections," which only flourish in large, centralized populations, were not part of the "human evolutionary experience because they either kill or induce solid immunity" (Bloomfield et al., 2016). Epidemiological research conducted in Finland, Denmark, and the United Kingdom confirm that these infectious diseases do not protect against allergic diseases, making Rook's "Old Friends" hypothesis more widely recognized by microbiologists (Bloomfield et al., 2016).

Understanding the "Old Friends" Hypothesis in the Context of Environmental Mismatches

Rook's "Old Friends" hypothesis proposes how environmental mismatches between hunter-gatherer societies in the Neolithic age and urbanization in a high-income country can limit the exposure to "old friends." First, the advent of medical, hygiene, and sanitation practices have reduced the presence of "old friends" infections. Most notably, the depletion of historic infections can be seen with the introduction of antibiotics in the 1950s and the subsequent trend toward over prescription (Rook et al., 2014). With antibiotics inducing bacterial cell death, research has found that antibiotics permanently alter the gut microbiota and result in an acute pro-inflammatory immune response (Cully, 2019). This link has been proven in a 2014 review of 50 epidemiological studies that show that excessive antibiotic use, particularly in early childhood, strongly correlates with an increased risk of allergic disease (Bloomfield et al., 2016).

Additionally, the most critical times for "old friends" exposure are early in development, during pregnancy, delivery, and the first few days or months of infancy (Bloomfield et al., 2016). With modern advancements leading toward Caesarean deliveries, research has found that newborns delivered by C-section lack strains of vital gut bacteria and contain harmful opportunistic bacteria that are unique to hospitals (Callaway, 2019). Even the transfer of bacteria through breastfeeding has a large influence on the gut microbiome, and thus shifts in the feeding patterns of infants have long-term implications for the development of allergies (Pannaraj et al., 2019). While more research is needed to confirm any association with allergic disease, key cultural shifts in the treatment of children have resulted in the drastic depletion of the gut microbiome.

Lastly, as cities become more urbanized, infants are in less contact with the animals and green spaces of a "rural microbiome" during the first two-three years of life (Zou et al., 2018). As a result, the gut microbial ecosystem is severely depleted, which is associated with increased allergic sensitization (Rook et al., 2014). Thus, as more humans have drastically shifted their lifestyle from the Neolithic age to the modern urbanized era, the decrease in exposure to microorganisms that co-evolved with humans has resulted in weaker immune responses to foreign antigens.

The Hygiene Hypothesis and COVID-19

Without properly understanding why the "Hygiene Hypothesis" has been surpassed by more successful theories, parents may end up exposing their children to dangerous pathogens (including SARS-CoV-2) with misguided, good intentions. Through the lens of the "Old Friends" hypothesis, the public perception of being "too clean in our own homes" remains unfounded in the face of current research. An explosion of data obtained using RNA sequencing of samples from US homes suggests that modern homes are "teeming with microbes" (Bloomfield et al., 2016). With studies confirming that effective personal hygiene can kill dangerous pathogens, environmental bacteria from outside and commensal bacteria from other people provide households with microbiota (Bin Abdulrahman et al., 2019). Additionally, Rook's "Old Friends" hypothesis argues that "crowd infections," such as measles and the common cold appeared far too late in our evolutionary history to play a critical role in developing our immune system. Thus, public belief that exposing children to COVID-19 by abandoning lockdown measures and safety guidelines improves immune response puts children in a dangerous position. Instead, making sure that kids are properly vaccinated, have enough time to play outside, and follow COVID-19 safety guidelines have been widely accepted by the scientific community to be the best way to protect the immune health of children (Moyer, 2020).

Conclusion

Since the advent of the Hygiene Hypothesis in 1989, researchers have gained a broader understanding of the relationship between human immunity and bacterial/parasitic symbionts. However, further research needs to be conducted to understand how the COVID-19 pandemic will retrain our immune systems. Longitudinal studies comparing disease incidence between children of previous generations to current "COVID babies" may provide the key link to understand how shifts in behavioral patterns contribute to the health of our immune system. However, despite the exciting research possibilities, one concept remains certain: dangerously exposing ourselves to the SARS-CoV-2 virus will not strengthen our immune systems. On the contrary, practicing strict lockdown measures, routine hygiene practices, and getting vaccinated are vital in ending this pandemic, once and for all.

Works Cited

Alexandre-Silva, G. M., Brito-Souza, P. A., Oliveira, A. C. S., Cerni, F. A., Zottich, U., & Pucca, M. B. (2018). "The hygiene hypothesis at a glance: Early exposures, immune mechanism and novel therapies." *Acta Tropica*, 188, 16–26. https://doi.org/10.1016/j.actatropica.2018.08.032

Atarashi, K., Tanoue, T., Oshima, K., Suda, W., Nagano, Y., Nishikawa, H., Fukuda, S., Saito, T., Narushima, S., Hase, K., Kim, S., Fritz, J. V., Wilmes, P., Ueha, S., Matsushima, K., Ohno, H., Olle, B., Sakaguchi, S., Taniguchi, T., Honda, K. (2013). "Treg induction by a rationally selected mixture of Clostridia strains from the human microbiota." *Nature*, 500 (7461), 232–236. https://doi.org/10.1038/nature12331

Bach, J.-F. (2018). "The hygiene hypothesis in autoimmunity: The role of pathogens and commensals." *Nature Reviews Immunology*, 18(2), 105–120. https://doi.org/10.1038/nri.2017.111

Berger, A. (2000). Th1 and Th2 responses: What are they? *BMJ : British Medical Journal, 321* (7258), 424.

Bloomfield, S. F., Rook, G. A., Scott, E. A., Shanahan, F., Stanwell-Smith, R., & Turner, P. (2016). "Time to abandon the hygiene hypothesis: New perspectives on allergic disease, the human microbiome, infectious disease prevention and the role of targeted hygiene." *Perspectives in Public Health, 136*(4), 213–224. https://doi.org/10.1177/1757913916650225

Cepon-Robins, T. J., & Gildner, T. E. (2020). "Old friends meet a new foe." *Evolution, Medicine, and Public Health, 2020*(1), 234–248. https://doi.org/10.1093/emph/eoaa037

Charles A Janeway, J., Travers, P., Walport, M., & Shlomchik, M. J. (2001). "Immunological Memory." *Immunobiology: The Immune System in Health and Disease. 5th Edition*. https://www.ncbi.nlm.nih.gov/books/NBK27158/

Chatterjee, B., Karandikar, R. L., & Mande, S. C. (2020). "The mortality due to COVID-19 in different nations is associated with the demographic character of nations and the prevalence of autoimmunity." *MedRxiv*, 2020.07.31.20165696. https://doi.org/10.1101/2020.07.31.20165696

Cully, M. (2019). "Antibiotics alter the gut microbiome and host health." *Nature Research*. https://doi.org/10.1038/d42859-019-00019-x

Moyer, M. W. (2020, September 10). "Is Staying Home Harming Your Child's Immune System?" *The New York Times*. https://www.nytimes.com/2020/09/10/parenting/children-immunity-staying-home-coronavirus.html

National Center for Biotechnology Information. (2020). "The innate and adaptive immune systems." *InformedHealth.org [Internet]*. Institute for Quality and Efficiency in Health Care (IQWiG). https://www.ncbi.nlm.nih.gov/books/NBK279396/

Ragab, D., Salah Eldin, H., Taeimah, M., Khattab, R., & Salem, R. (2020). "The COVID-19 Cytokine Storm; What We Know So Far." *Frontiers in Immunology, 11*. https://doi.org/10.3389/fimmu.2020.01446

Rook, G. A. W., Raison, C. L., & Lowry, C. A. (2014). "Microbial 'old friends', immunoregulation and socioeconomic status."*Clinical and Experimental Immunology, 177* (1), 1–12. https://doi.org/10.1111/cei.12269

Scudellari, M. (2017). "News Feature: Cleaning up the hygiene hypothesis." *Proceedings of the National Academy of Sciences, 114* (7), 1433–1436. https://doi.org/10.1073/pnas.1700688114

Stiemsma, L., Reynolds, L., Turvey, S., & Finlay, B. (2015). "The hygiene hypothesis: Current perspectives and future therapies." *ImmunoTargets and Therapy*, 143. https://doi.org/10.2147/ITT.S61528

von Mutius, E. (2007). "Allergies, infections and the hygiene hypothesis—The epidemiological evidence." *Immunobiology*, 212 (6), 433–439. https://doi.org/10.1016/j.imbio.2007.03.002

von Mutius, E. (2010). "99th Dahlem Conference on Infection, Inflammation and Chronic Inflammatory Disorders: Farm lifestyles and the hygiene hypothesis." *Clinical and Experimental Immunology*, 160, 130–135. https://doi.org/10.1111/j.1365-2249.2010.04138.x

The Zelda Provenzano Endowed STEM Writing Award

Emma Barnes

The Fast and the Fashionable: How Your Closet Contributes to a Global Crisis

A world in ruin. Millions of crumbling, steaming sweatshop factories. In them: children and mothers aching to achieve impossible production targets. Plastic the length of continents individually wrapping conveyors of identical t-shirts. Carbon emissions seeping—no, flooding—into a fragile atmosphere under a boiling sun. All of this for what? For the teens of today to snap one Instagram picture in their new, trendy outfit, then never wear it again. The horrors of capitalism are stitched into the fabric on our backs, and it goes by the name "fast fashion." This concept is characterized by rapid prototyping of in-season styles, leading to large-scale, cheap production. To the (typically younger) consumer base, fast fashion seems like a dream: high end on a low budget. Contrarily, the too-good-to-be-true prices have created global and inhumane enterprises like Forever 21, UNIQLO, ASOS, Primark, H&M, and Gap. It is no surprise that these highly profitable markets have taken off this decade considering humans purchase 400% more clothing than they did twenty years ago (Hart et al 9). This rise in unethical consumerism must be tackled head-on with more sustainable alternatives, as the path we are on will leave us helpless within much of the current population's lifetime. Our maladaptive notion of fast fashion is debilitating to both workers' rights and environmental safety, after which these clothes occupy landfills with as little as one wear. The prescribed solution of thrifting, while it has conversely robbed low-income solutions for a quality wardrobe, is one of many paths we must turn to before it is too late.

The most inhumane aspect of this phenomenon is the outsourced labor which suffers underpaid, demanding, and hazardous work environments to meet the commands of privileged buyers. According to the *2019 Ethical Fashion Report*, worker empowerment was the "lowest scoring section, with a median grade of D" on a scale of A-F (9). As our tags typically imply, an enormous amount of clothing is produced overseas from where it is typically bought; even the better brands like Zara "outsource at least 13 percent of their manufacturing to China and Turkey" (Joy et al 275). The obvious reason fast fashion moguls seek foreign production is the same reason any business makes any decision: it's cheaper. In Bangladesh—home of the cheapest labor force—the living wage is "2.8 times its current minimum wage," which most workers still fail to receive (Hart et al 19). Only 5% of 130 analyzed brands could claim to provide a living wage for all employees as of 2019, a disgusting figure for the modern day (Hart et al 11). Because of this poor compensation, employees must often work "12 to 16 hours a day, and regularly 80 hours a week," in addition to forced overtime based on demanding targets for the high-demand industry (Alam and Hearson 4). These targets also support the use of short-term contracts with factory laborers that may be easily hired or fired to "adjust to fluctuations in production needs" (Stafford). There exists a gross hypocrisy of privileged consumers who can afford higher-priced, sustainable items that instead buy from corporations that prop up labor-wage abuse to increase their own profits. If someone had to suffer to produce the shirt on your back, would it give a new perspective to the impressive deals you see on the market? Are the couple of dollars you save on a shirt worth another human's safety? If that astonishingly low price seems too good to be true, it likely is.

Beyond crises of humanity, a climate crisis has arisen as a result of the fashion industry's wasteful production, delivery methods, and carbon emissions, proving it to be highly unsustainable for the future. As more buyers become aware of their impact, 86% of the general population believes that social and environmental issues should be addressed by the fashion industry—with 94% of Gen Z agreeing to the same proposition (Hart et al 22). However, a paradox presents itself in that "only 31 percent of Gen-Z and just 12 percent of baby boomers" are willing to pay more for sustainably produced fashion (Amed et al 52). Again, privilege takes hold of consumer preferences. When the fashion industry "accounts for 20 to 35 percent of microplastic" in our oceans, privilege should not prevail (Amed et al 52). In addition to polluting the world's water, these brands also consume our fresh water in vast, unsustainable quantities. To make a single cotton t-shirt, 2,700 liters of fresh water is required, contributing to the 79 billion cubic meters used every year on fashion alone (Hart et al 9). Additionally, considering the apparel industry is responsible for 10% of carbon emissions globally, action must be taken now to reduce this consumer bingeing, or it will not support us much longer (Hart et al 9). Some companies even cheat these net emission statistics through carbon offsetting—funding third parties to reduce carbon emissions elsewhere—without actually changing their production methods (Amed et al 54). As all these figures continue to rise, it is important to consider that the more we waste our resources now, the shorter we will have access to them, and the more desperate the human situation will become over time. There will come a day when our current way of life will no longer be sustainable, but until then, we must alter our consumer behavior to prolong and strengthen our natural resources. A new outfit for every occasion should not trump the fate of your children on a warming planet with little to drink.

The environment also suffers due to landfill contribution and poor recycling, propagated by the concept of micro-seasons and impulsive consumer behavior. Of the "53 million tons of fiber [produced] every year… more than 70 percent of that ends up in landfills or on bonfires" instead of being put to reuse or recycling initiatives—mainly because few exist (Amed et al 56). Australia as a country discards "6,000 kg of fashion and textile waste every ten minutes" according to the *2019 Ethical Fashion Report*, with most of that also ending up in landfills (9). We must identify the factors that label the fast fashion industry "a fast-response system that encourages disposability" (Joy et al 275). The root of this issue stems in part from the short-term gratification that trendy and seasonal clothing offers. UC Berkeley's premier undergraduate economics journal claims that there existed "11 to 52 [fashion] seasons a year by 2014," rather than the winter, spring, summer, fall cycles many believe we still follow (Nair). To keep up with the rapid fashion tastes changing, "H&M and Forever 21 receive new garment shipments every day… Topshop features 400 new styles every week, while Zara releases 20,000 designs annually," dubbing the fast fashion giants "heralds of mass consumerism" (Stafford). The turnover for these clothes is so dramatic that it is no wonder the people who crave modernity of style would also be those to discard more quickly at the end of the trend—that is, if it survives that long. The other factor that propagates mass disposal of fast fashion is the poor quality, reflected by the pricing and mass production. As stated in peer-reviewed journal *Fashion Theory*, a consumer "may keep an item after ten washes, but the item may lose its luster by then," giving rise to the "ten-washes" colloquialism common to fast fashion (283). This rapid distaste and degradation of the fast fashion industry is not sustainable so long as we continue to pile landfills with fabric that may be used to provide more than ten wears (if that).

The most common solution to mass disposal of clothing also presents itself as an alternative to fast fashion shopping: thrift stores. While second-hand buying seems like a guilt-free, stimulating practice in a movement toward sustainability, an influx of eager consumers does not bode well for the low-income communities that rely on these stores for simple necessities. Prior to a large-scale awareness of sustainability issues, thrift stores carried "strong taboos of uncleanliness and poverty," making it difficult for people to shop for less money without being stigmatized by people with a more comfortable income (Nair). Now their critics are coming to find "deals" at local thrift stores, stealing the opportunity from those who need the better price points. The sale-hungry consumers also tend to possess the "time-flexibility of being able to visit these stores soon after they are restocked, which working individuals simply do not have," further infringing on the opportunity of low-income shoppers (Nair). Additionally, "the poor are disproportionately more obese than the rich" and often need to search for larger sizes in these stores; the current setting for thrifting is that thinner bodies buy oversized outfits and tailor them to fit (Nair). The opposite is much less practical for larger individuals that need the clothing in its original state. Contrary to the initial purpose of reducing clothing purchases, the high transactional utility of getting an object for a steeply discounted price is also prone to result in a greater amount of purchases for the same cost they would have spent on a more sustainable choice instead. The irony and privilege prevalent in thrifting culture makes it seem like picking between two evils: infringe on the rights of workers abroad or the low-income consumers in our communities.

Although, the reality is that supporting local thrift stores has many positive points as well, making it the best modern alternative. For prices similar to the appeal of fast fashion and for the sustainability beyond all first-hand buying, second-hand buying continues to be most effective. An increase in attendance of second-hand stores also promotes the donation of materials for further reuse. This angle also seeks to resolve the issue of clothing in landfills and scrap warehouses where reuse is exponentially less likely. Many non-profits like Goodwill and Housing Works also "reinvest into the development of poor communities," meaning supporting these stores has the potential to bring up the communities that need them to the point where cheap clothing is not a last resort for the lower ends of society (Nair). Given the shortcomings of second-hand buying, the greater good is being served against fast fashion toward a more sustainable future while also protecting foreign exploitation and the environment through thrift stores.

The timeline for a change of our buying habits is rapidly becoming shorter as we dig ourselves into the hole of irreparable damage. The world won't unmelt the ice caps or reverse the depletion of the ozone layer. Overseas factory workers won't forget the violence and labor abuse they suffer. Their starving families will not be suddenly fed. Sustainability of buying habits is something we must practice immediately—not just claim to uphold. This is the year we research brands and their policies before prioritizing our wardrobes over a long-term, sustainable market; choose Adidas, Hanes, and Patagonia over Nike, Abercrombie & Fitch, and Ralph Lauren, and shop from small businesses instead of unethical corporate schemes. We cannot continue to value our bank accounts and fashion trends more than our future. Before impulse-buying your next wardrobe piece, ask yourself: is our privilege now worth our humanity later?

Works Cited

Alam, Khorshed, and Martin Hearson. "Fashion Victims: The True Cost of Cheap Clothes at Primark, Asda, and Tesco." *War on Want*, Dec. 2006.

Amed, Imran, et al. *The State of Fashion 2020*. McKinsey & Company, 20 Nov. 2019.

Hart, Clair, et al. *The 2019 Ethical Fashion Report: The Truth Behind the Barcode*. Baptist World Aid Australia, Apr. 2019.

Joy, Annamma, et al. "Fast Fashion, Sustainability, and the Ethical Appeal of Luxury Brands." *Fashion Theory 16.3*, 2012, p 273-295.

Nair, Nanditha. "Rise of Thrifting: Solution to Fast Fashion or Stealing from the Poor?" *Berkeley Economic Review*, edited by Abhishek Roy, 19 Nov. 2019, econreview.berkeley.edu/rise-of-thrifting-solution-to-fast-fashion-or-stealing-from-the-poor/.

Stafford, Victoria. "Factory Exploitation and the Fast Fashion Machine." *Green America*, 8 Aug. 2018, greenamerica.org/blog/factory-exploitation-and-fast-fashion-machine.

The Zelda Provenzano Endowed STEM Writing Award

María José Garcia

What About Us? Scientific, Technological, and Health Disparities

I was battling with the cold Philadelphia wind on my way to class when I received a call from my mother. It was January 2020 and I had just left Honduras a few days ago. After inquiring about my sleeping schedule and eating habits, my mother made a bizarre request. Before saying goodbye, she told me to go buy hand sanitizer and face masks because there was a virus going around. Though I had heard about the COVID-19 virus in Wuhan, China, I did not pay much attention to my mother's cautionary tale. In fact, I did not buy hand sanitizer or face masks. Little did I know that over a year later those items would be in demand and we would have more than 137 million COVID-19 cases, and more than 2.95 million deaths worldwide. In those first few months of uncertainty and worldwide chaos, I was stranded in the United States. After months, I was able to return home to Honduras. Having experienced this public health crisis in two extremely different settings I began to wonder why public health recommendations and scientific advancements were well received in some settings and useless in others. In my attempt to understand, I encountered historical account after historical account of the massive scientific, technological, and health disparities exacerbated by innovations that cannot be used in low socioeconomic settings. The purpose of this piece is to bring awareness of these inequities in such a critical time. I do not intend to burden the scientific community with an issue that pertains to multiple sectors of our society. Rather, I aim to encourage and highlight the responsibility current and future scientists have, not only to curve human suffering through means of innovation but to create technological advancements that can be enjoyed by many regardless of their socioeconomic status.

The scientific world is incredibly rich and as technological advancements become integral parts of our daily lives, who is a scientist and what they do is defined and explored in different manners depending on who you are asking. For this essay, we will follow the Science Council's definition. A scientist is someone who "systematically gathers and uses research and evidence, to make hypotheses and test them, to gain and share understanding and knowledge." Though the definition is relatively broad, it encapsulates a wide range of curious individuals with a wide range of qualifications that contribute and make a significant change to the world as we know it. A limited view of who can be considered a scientist and what they do makes it easier for people across fields to discount their responsibility of going beyond the traditional expectations of their industries to achieve more equitable access to their innovations. A more diverse perspective allows everyone across ages and backgrounds to be exposed to a wide range of disciplines and conversations that otherwise would be disregarded as mere curious thoughts.

Scientists, especially those in the healthcare sector, have a great influence not only on how society functions, but in poverty reduction and the improvement of quality of life (World Health Organization). These influences, however, do not solely rely upon the innovations themselves, but the intent with which the innovations were created and who can access them. Singer, in his piece "The Technology Gap and the Developing Countries" emphasizes how wealthy, developed countries "… have different interests, different problems and seek different solutions than those in the developing countries." As least developed countries (LDCs) become more dependent on technologies and advancements created and developed in wealthy countries, it becomes clear that the accumulation of useful information and technology generates more obstacles in the implementation of such innovations in low resource areas. Though these innovations might be ideal in some settings or represent significant advancements in the scientific world, they are rendered useless in other settings. Fekitamoeloa 'Utoikamanu, the United Nations Under-Secretary-General and High Representative for the Least Developed Countries, in her piece "Closing the Technology Gap in Least Developed Countries", points out that as technology advances many are left behind "… due to the political, economic and social consequences of rapidly expanding inequality."

Singer explored these technological disparities in 1970, and more than 50 years later the issue has not only increased but has driven low-income communities to use obsolete technologies since the current innovations are years away from being accessible. We cannot deny that impressive technological leaps are being made but as 'Utoikamanu points out, "… the economic and social benefits remain geographically concentrated, primarily in developed countries." As scientists around the world discuss their approaches on how to solve a certain ailment, low resource settings, and LDCs are left behind or completely excluded from the conversation. The passion and need to solve a problem, cure a disease, or simply make a scientific breakthrough takes precedence over the practicality of its implementation and its accessibility. Though we cannot ignore the governance and economic issues that influence the structural deficiencies of these low-income settings, it would be disingenuous to say that scientists can simply create solutions without thinking about the communities they would be impacting. Scientists have a responsibility to acknowledge that the way they approach a problem may affect who can access their solution in the long run.

In 1969 the United Nations released a World Plan of Action for the Application of Science and Technology to Development where they explore and highlight the influence and responsibility developed countries have to help bridge the technological gap in LDCs. They emphasize how there is a need "…to attempt to change the composition of the stock of knowledge so that it is relevant to the developing countries" (United Nations, 1969, para 101). In other words, developed countries must reorganize and repurpose resources of science and technology towards the creation of products and innovations that are particularly relevant to LDCs. Though the investment in research and development efforts for LDCs is important, it is not sustainable without the cooperation and social awareness of scientists. The plan highlights how the effective coupling of scientists across national and cultural boundaries proves key to the efficient functioning of science and technology (United Nations, 1969, para. 53). The connection, communication, and overall awareness of scientists in developed countries with the experiences and knowledge of scientists and professionals in low-income communities establish critical advantages in the accumulation of scientific knowledge.

The United Nations 1969's World Plan of Action is relevant to our discussion considering that decades later the organization keeps giving the same recommendations and the countries involved keep committing to the same overall principles. In the World Plan of Action, it is acknowledged there is a substantial international division regarding the magnitude and spectrum of science, technology, and innovation (STI). Currently, 'Utoikamanu and the United Nations make the same argument. With the 2030 Sustainable Development Goals (SDGs) and the pledge to Leave No One Behind, countries around the world have committed to a global partnership to bring peace and prosperity for people and the planet. Although we speak about countries, developed and developing, it is key to note that the creativity, knowledge, and commitment from all societies and individuals across the world is necessary to achieve the SDGs in every context. The SDG number 10 focuses on reducing inequalities within and among countries and scientists have been key not only in the advising but in the creation of the steps to be taken to achieve a more equitable society. That responsibility and awareness scientists have is key in bridging the technological gap and considering accessibility when designing solutions. The United Nations General Assembly appointed 15 experts representing a variety of backgrounds, scientific disciplines, and institutions, to author The Global Sustainable Development Report in 2019. The acknowledgment and emphasis that scientists from different cultural and socioeconomic backgrounds contribute significantly to solutions of problems that affect us all highlight the importance of creating social awareness in the scientific community. The geographical, cultural, and gender balance in scientific groups drives the realization that it is possible to create technological advancements that can be enjoyed by many regardless of their socioeconomic status.

Though we have highlighted the power dynamics and influence of wealthy countries over low-income ones, it is worth emphasizing that these socioeconomic disparities transcend geographical borders. Scientists indeed have great influence in the creation of public policy and international relations, but their expertise, advice, and innovations affect individuals regardless of their nationalities as well. The need to encourage and highlight the responsibility current and future scientists have, not only to curve human suffering through means of innovation but to create technological advancements that benefit people regardless of their socioeconomic status, has become increasingly important in the last year. As the SDG number 10 highlights, inequalities, especially in healthcare, do not occur solely across borders. The COVID-19 pandemic has revealed how deeply ingrained these disparities are in our society. Within the United States, a country that encourages scientific thinking and hosts numerous world-renowned scientific institutions, there is increasing evidence that certain racial and ethnic minority groups have been disproportionately affected by COVID-19 (CDC, 2021 para. 2). However, even before the pandemic, journals such as the *Association of American Medical*

Colleges published articles about health disparities based on socioeconomic inequities.

Dr. Fiscella, an associate professor in the Departments of Family Medicine and Community Preventive Medicine at the University of Rochester School of Medicine and Dentistry, explores this phenomenon in his 2004 article called "Health Disparities Based on Socioeconomic Inequities: Implications for Urban Health Care." In this article, he highlights how health is unevenly distributed across socioeconomic status. These factors, and not genetics, are the main cause of these health disparities (Fiscella, 2004). Health disparities resulting from socioeconomic status become apparent early in a person's life cycle and can have long-lasting effects. "By adulthood, health disparities related to socioeconomic status are striking. Compared with persons who have a college education, those with less than a high school education have life expectancies that are six years shorter" (Fiscella, 2004, para. 10). In a world where income and education determine your life span, it is key for those in the scientific community to become aware that health goes beyond the disease and as such we must create technological advancements that do not become obsolete depending on what geographical space you place it.

More than a decade after Dr. Fiscella's study, during the COVID-19 pandemic, these socioeconomic disparities and the overrepresentation of minority groups in death counts have been exacerbated to such an extent that scientists' roles have become essential in not only curing the disease but making sure their innovations do not worsen and expand these inequalities. "As the rate of scientific advancement to fight COVID-19 moves quickly, COVID-19 disparities are likely to increase, as we observed during the U.S. H1N1 influenza pandemic" (Galaviz et al., 2020). As history highlights time and time again, it has become increasingly clear scientists have a responsibility to at least be aware and try to create technological advancements that can be enjoyed by many regardless of their socioeconomic status. If this social awareness does not become an integral part of the research and creation process of technological advancement, we run the risk of sacrificing the most vulnerable for the sake of scientific breakthroughs.

Critics of the idea of having social awareness at the forefront of the scientific research cycle and the creation process of innovations do not oppose acknowledging the responsibility scientists have with those in vulnerable socioeconomic status. Instead, they raise concerns about the unique challenges addressing these inequalities pose and the need for more funding. Concerns are raised about delaying the release of scientific innovations or having additional constraints in the creation of technological advancements. However, the purpose of encouraging scientists to implement research techniques that reduce health disparities is not to deter or delay scientific developments, rather it is a way of refocusing these efforts. Mercedes Carnethon, the vice-chair of the Department of Preventive Medicine in Northwestern University, and her colleagues highlight in their article "Disparities Research, Disparities Researchers, and Health Equity" how the world's largest funder of biomedical research, the US National Institutes of Health (NIH), "supports a suite of research and career development programs designed to eliminate health disparities. Despite the clear message from the NIH that health disparities are a significant concern, the scientific community has not embraced the message." Though the scientific community acknowledges to a certain extent that health disparities are an issue, there is a need to amplify this message. Therefore, as we continue battling with the COVID-19 pandemic and countries around the world invest in technological advancements to curb the spread of the disease, there is a need to implement strategies that acknowledge and work with existing health inequalities.

Implementation science offers approaches that can help understand the factors driving these disparities. These approaches help design interventions that can reach and are suitable in minority communities and low-income settings. "…Implementation frameworks can be used to understand historical context, values, culture, and needs of minority populations. Behavioral approaches can be used to identify drivers of health behavior and inform the design of interventions" (Galaviz et al., 2020). These approaches can be used by scientists and innovators to design interventions for improving recommendations on how to shelter in place, mask-wearing, and physical distancing behaviors among minority populations. There are existing frameworks focused on the equitable implementation, participation, and design of interventions (Galaviz et al., 2020). Whether it is on an individual basis or a health-system level, there are design tool guides to enhance the relevance and impact of upcoming, new interventions. Implementation science offers approaches that acknowledge and guide scientists when dealing with disparity-sensitive design, distribution, and implementation of innovations and interventions in low-income communities. To echo the United Nations SDGs pledge, Leave No One Behind.

"Testing and refining of interventions should be guided by comprehensive sociodemographic data to ensure the feasibility of implementation, enhance relevance, and improve the effectiveness of interventions across racial and ethnic minorities" (Galaviz et al., 2020). The scientific, technological, and health disparities have not only increased due to the rate at which scientific developments are happening. As scientists and innovators revisit, redesign, and repurpose existing inventions, it is necessary they also take into consideration sociodemographic data to ensure these wonderful scientific developments are not rendered useless and obsolete in low socioeconomic areas. Highlighting the responsibility scientists have to create solutions and innovations that can be enjoyed by anyone regardless of their socioeconomic background does not mean that scientists are the sole contributor to these health disparities. Instead, it means that scientists that successfully address and do not exacerbate these health disparities, ensure that "…not only the most vulnerable but also all individuals have access to, and benefit from, quality health care and public health interventions" (Galaviz et al., 2020).

For instance, the idea of future scientists and innovators acknowledging the responsibility of creating accessible solutions can be exemplified by a team of biomedical engineering students at John Hopkins University. They developed a low-cost device to treat postpartum hemorrhage in low-resource settings. Instead of shying away from the unique challenges low-resource settings present, they embraced and worked with the limitations. Postpartum hemorrhage is the leading cause of maternal mortality worldwide, however, "the disparity between low- and high-resource settings is massive, with 99% of hemorrhage-related mortality occurring in developing countries" (Hu et al., 2020). Postpartum hemorrhages are treatable. However, the recommended intervention poses significant obstacles to clinicians in low resource settings since it uses ultrasound and other imaging modalities that they do not have access to (Hu et al., 2020). These students, committed to creating an accessible solution, developed a device that does not require the use of ultrasound or other expensive technology. They worked alongside experienced faculty members and clinical mentors to help them understand the root cause of the problem and how to address it while keeping in mind the need for a low-cost solution and the barriers in low-income settings. These students did not only make an effort to curve human suffering through means of innovation but aimed to create technological advancements accessible to vulnerable people in our society.

It is time to believe that the scientific community has the power to contribute to the reduction of the scientific, technological, and health disparities we are currently facing. Whether it is across borders or within our own, let the COVID-19 pandemic be the start of a worldwide effort to reduce and not exacerbate these inequalities. As countries and institutions around the world invest in solutions and interventions to slow the spread and cure the disease, let's take the United Nation's SDGs to heart and pledge alongside them to leave no one behind. Let's encourage current and future scientists to create solutions that can be enjoyed by anyone regardless of socioeconomic status. Rather than burdening the scientific community with such a complex and multifactorial issue, let's empower each other with the notion that taking into consideration these disparities from day one in our research cycle and design process can make a significant change in the world.

Works Cited

Carnethon, M., Kershaw, K., & Kandula, N. (2019). "Disparities Research, Disparities Researchers, and Health Equity." *JAMA: The Journal of the American Medical Association*, 323(3), 211–212. https://doi.org/10.1001/jama.2019.19329

Centers for Disease Control and Prevention. "Health Equity Considerations and Racial and Ethnic Minority Groups. Centers for Disease Control and Prevention." https://www.cdc.gov/coronavirus/2019-ncov/community/health-equity/race-ethnicity.html.

Fiscella, Kevin MD, MPH; Williams, David R. Ph.D., MPH "Health Disparities Based on Socioeconomic Inequities: Implications for Urban Health Care." *Academic Medicine*, December 2004—Volume 79—Issue 12—p 1139-1147.

Fiscella K., Franks P., Gold M.R., Clancy C.M. "Inequality in Quality: addressing socioeconomic, racial, and ethnic disparities in health care." *JAMA*. 2000;283:2579–84.

Galaviz, Karla I., Jessica Y. Breland, Mechelle Sanders, Khadijah Breathett, Alison Cerezo, Oscar Gil, John M. Hollier, Cassondra Marshall, J. Deanna Wilson, & Utibe R Essien. (2020). "Implementation Science to Address Health Disparities During the Coronavirus Pandemic." *Health Equity*, 4(1), 463–467. https://doi.org/10.1089/heq.2020.0044

Hopkins BME, "Students Develop Low-Cost Device to Treat Hostpartum hemorrhage in Low-Resource Settings." *Johns Hopkins Biomedical Engineering*. https://www.bme.jhu.edu/news-events/news/hopkins-bme-students-develop-low-cost-device-to-treat-postpartum-hemorrhage-in-low-resource-settings/

Hu, K., Lapinski, M., Mischler, G., Allen, R., Manbachi, A., & Seay, R. (2020). "Improved Treatment of Postpartum Hemorrhage: Design, Development, and Bench-Top Validation of a Reusable

Intrauterine Tamponade Device for Low-Resource Settings." *Journal of Medical Devices*, 14(1). https://doi.org/10.1115/1.4045965

Our Definition of a Scientist. (2020, March 3). https://sciencecouncil.org/about-science/our-definition-of-a-scientist.

Rohman, M. (2020, January 22). "Funding Disparities Research and Underrepresented Minority Scientists." *News Center*. https://news.feinberg.northwestern.edu/2020/01/funding-disparities-research-and-underrepresented-minority-scientists/

Singer, H. W.(1972) "The Technology Gap and the Developing Countries." *International Journal of Environmental Studies*, 3:1-4, 119-123, DOI: 10.1080/00207237208709502

United Nations. Sustainable Development Goals. *UNDP*. https://www.undp.org/content/undp/en/home/sustainable-development-goals.html.

United Nations. (1969). *World plan of action for the application of science and technology to development, note by the Secretary-General, draft of introductory statement prepared by a group of consultants* (Rep.)

United Nations. (2019). *Global Sustainable Development Report* (Rep.)

Utoikamanu, F. "Closing the Technology Gap in the least Developed Countries. United Nations." *https://www.un.org/en/chronicle/article/closing-technology-gap-least-developed-countries.*

Drexel Publishing Group

Creative Writing
___

Introduction

The following creative works were selected by faculty judges from student submissions (of creative nonfiction, fiction, humor, op-ed, and poetry) to the Drexel Publishing Group Creative Writing Contest. There were many strong entries in all categories. These pieces engage with issues of culture, love, identity, and the difficulties of becoming an adult. They are as diverse as the students who wrote them. These writers may make you laugh, make you cry, and make you think. You may marvel at the insight, humor, and humanity these writers possess. These writers are brave and generous in their desire to share their work. Please enjoy the writing they shared.

—*The Editors*

First Place—Creative Nonfiction

Max Gallagher
Cough Into My Open Mouth

Everybody in my lecture hall is sick. Every lull in the lesson is occupied by a wet sniffle, the end of every phrase interrupted by a suppressed yet productive cough. Even my own sinuses consider weeping in sympathy, urging me to match the pitch of the surrounding ensemble, to ooze in harmony. The class stumbles through conversions from binary to decimal to hex, and back to binary, but I am past stumbling. I want to move on, or at least progress without tripping, without being interrupted by another suckling snuff.

My roommate got sick, but he didn't sniffle. He was feverish and his throat hurt. It was a more noble sickness than the noisy and shameless children that enclose me. He went to sleep early, earlier than his typical 2 a.m. bedtime—and I put a wet cloth on his forehead. Before he fell asleep, I kissed his cheek, and I told him that I loved him. He snored lightly and I listened to it as I drifted. When he awoke, he told me that he loved me, and he kissed my lips.

In the subsequent days, we didn't talk very much. Being around him made my lips sting and my eyes cloudy and my chest ache. Breaking the silence, he told me that we should go back to being friends, only friends, nothing more. But his scent filled every pore on my body and diffused into my memories. But I thought about holding him while we slept, kissing him in the dark—away from the windows where anybody might see us. But I couldn't stop thinking about the inference I hadn't realized I made.

He cared about me; this is certain. He smiled when I looked at him, and he held my hand when we were alone. It felt like love. We hid under my sheets, whispering so quietly that even we couldn't hear. He touched his nose to mine while we kissed. It felt like love. All the evidence and facts told me that this was love. If everything we had was collected into some grand exhibit, people from around the world would come and say, "Man, I want a love like that." It felt like a movie. My mistake was interpreting an inference—the many inferences I had made—as fact.

The facts are as follows: he and I no longer kiss each other. We don't sleep in the same bed, and we don't talk about our future anymore. We still stare at each other, but now instead of looking for pleasure we are analyzing, both trying to see who may break first. I could draw more inferences, and I could probably convince myself that he might come back, that I could wait for him infinitely, that he would ever want me the way I hated wanting him.

I try not to think about the future, one in which he almost loves me again. It's more painful to imagine that he could ever reciprocate than to think about losing him completely.

Maybe if we really loved each other it could happen. Maybe if we weren't in college. Maybe if we weren't roommates. *Roommates.* I still see him every day. He still snores slightly, still grinds his teeth for a second or two when he shifts his sleeping position, still looks at me like he cares, and still makes me need him. He's still sick, now starting to sniffle and cough like the rest of the world.

Somehow, I never was infected. His contaminated tongue ran along my teeth, down my throat and into my lungs. I inhaled his exhale, the air that somehow tasted like him. Somehow, I don't cough, I won't sniffle, and I rarely sneeze, but I know that I'm not healthy. Healthy people's hearts don't seize and burn. Healthy people don't feel the earth vibrating above their eyelids in every blink, and they don't feel an ocean under their seats, churning and threatening to drown them at any moment of uncertainty. There had always been uncertainty between us, and inferring love was favoring an uncomplicated ignorance, living in an optimistic, unrealistic fantasy. In the real world, love exists, or it doesn't. It is not something that can be inferred or intuited or interpreted. It is seen and felt, something that simply is.

When I try not to watch him move around our room at night, I don't know if he's going to hit me or kiss me, and both terrify me. Pretending that our relationship didn't change only works until we're alone and the sky is dark, what used to be our time to explore. I can still see the contours in his abdomen, the bones in his pelvis when he leaves the room fully clothed. I can smell the skin under his scent, the raw salt and sweat inside his savory, spiced aroma. My sheets smell like him. My mouth tastes like his. Infected and scared.

I start to feel healthier when I'm away, when I'm out of our room, our cave, our mausoleum. Even wilting away in overcrowded lecture halls is better than feeling entirely intangible in my home. The only thing worse than feeling nothing is feeling numb, and then briefly feeling happy, and then broken and numb, again.

There are occasional interludes when we feel correct. We revert to softer forms, returning to a friendship we used to share. We joke and touch the way that friends do, nothing more. It is warm and intimate, like we're hiding somewhere inside of *us* to play a secret game, one whose only rule is "don't give up on this." Then I'm standing right beside him, too scared to say that I miss him. Then we're both walking home alone though we're side by side, in phase, but sorely out of step. Then we're eating, asleep, and starting the day over again. Back to lecture, back to sickness, back to my health. Even my teacher is starting to sniffle now. I wonder if he's ever been in love.

Second Place—Creative Nonfiction

Anh Quach
Tales from Quarantine

1. *Cô.*

She was my seatmate on a repatriation flight full of Vietnamese people fleeing pandemic-stricken America. She looked anywhere between forty and sixty; I called her *cô*, or Auntie, as was customary in Vietnam. Her blue surgical mask hid everything from view: her smile, her features. Yet her nervousness remained palpable as she fidgeted, frantically sending last minute texts to her family and rearranging everything in her front seat pocket with near feverish zeal.

"My daughter was a student, too," she exclaimed upon learning I went to school in Philadelphia, "but she's gotten her green card."

Clinging to her seat as the plane reeled and shook during take-off, she told me about her daughter: how she went to college on a scholarship, how she was sponsored by a company for a well-paying position, how she bought a house, how she was living her American Dream. I watched her exhausted eyes sparkle with pride. I learned that her daughter had packed her suitcases, booked an expensive hotel room for her to quarantine in, and dropped her off at the airport that morning. I learned that she came to California to visit her daughter and had been stranded since COVID-19 began in March. I learned that she hadn't been outside ever since, and that I was the first Vietnamese person outside her family she had met.

Amid warm towelettes and cold snacks of ice cream and rice crackers, I learned that her husband fell ill while she was stranded.

"He didn't make it," she muttered. To herself. To the seat in front of her. To the half-eaten rice cracker in her lap. To no one in particular. She clumsily peeled open a towelette packet. She sank into her blanket. The empty middle seat expanded into a chasm. A sleepy passenger shut their window. Darkness enveloped, and her worried, weary eyes vanished. The plane thundered on. Loudly. Quietly. Mechanically.

"I'm sorry," was all I could mumble.

She reached for her bag. Her silhouette ransacked and dumped the content of the bag onto the empty middle seat packet after packet of Kit Kats, M&M's, you name it. She ran her hands through the candies as though they were her treasure trove, the only things she remembered to pack for the mass exodus.

"Help yourself," she said, piling candies onto my lap. My seat was suddenly alive and awash with heaps of sweets. *Cô* handed me a plastic bag to store them. "My daughter kept packing them," she complained. "How many times have I told her not to? She was worried I wouldn't have enough snacks in quarantine." Amid the darkness of a plane full of jet-lagged, long-suffering, exhausted people napping, I imagined her eyes again sparkling with pride. *Her daughter, the* poster child of the Vietnamese version of the American Dream, who cô wouldn't stop talking about even while fleeing America.

Seemingly re-energized, cô straightened up. With the same zeal I had seen her unload her candy bag, she chatted excitedly about pre-COVID California, the places she had visited, and the adventures she and her daughter had gone on before all hell broke loose. I saw her small frame reanimated as we ventured deeper into the realms of nostalgia. I pictured a smile underneath her mask. I watched as she momentarily stopped at every mention of the lockdown, shuddered, and quickly skirted the subject, as though dying to forget lockdowns and pandemics existed.

"Do well in school, okay?" she reminded me as the plane touched down. "What a privilege to be able to study in the US." How ironic of her to still be thinking about returning to the US while fleeing it.

Clutching her brimming bag, I watched her small frame disappear into the crowd of people disembarking the plane. I wanted to run to her, hug her, thank her for the candies, and let her know that *we were almost home*, but COVID-19 stopped me. Yet her long-suffering eyes haunted me still. I wondered what else she had been hiding underneath her surgical mask; what worries and anguish she had brought with her back home. I wondered what was going on in her and her daughter's minds.

We never said goodbye, I thought. I never knew her name.

2. Bạch Vân.

"It's hot out here today," said Bạch Vân, jumping clear of a gigantic water puddle.

She was my bunkmate in quarantine camp and quarantine best friend. Well-dressed, quiet, and sarcastic to a fault, she arrived with a myriad of boxes and suitcases seemingly too large to carry. Our bunks faced a window overlooking faraway mountain ranges surrounding a windy lawn where cows grazed. She and I spent a disproportionate amount of time indoors doing homework at odd hours and laughing at our ridiculous circumstances: that we never saw the beach despite being quarantined in a famous beach town, that power and water outages happened so regularly nobody would believe it, and that we had hung out so often in such close proximity that we would have practically given each other COVID-19—if both of us hadn't already caught it by then.

"Where did you live?" I asked her. We made our way through the perilous meanderings of a lawn littered with tree branches, toppled trees, and muddy puddles. The November sun scorched our eyes. Cracked windowpanes glittered from afar. A tropical cyclone had swept through the little beach town the night before.

"Outside of Seattle," she chuckled. "Nowhere, actually."

SEA to LAX to NRT to CXR. PHL to LAX to NRT to CXR. Two college students rescued home on near-identical flight itineraries yet blissfully oblivious of each other's existence. Funny how our paths only crossed thanks to quarantine camp and, strangely, COVID-19.

"I was in school for a few months," said Vân, kneeling, curiously examining a spindly uprooted tree. She hungrily dissected its bedraggled appearance. "Then COVID-19 happened, my school closed, and I've been stranded ever since."

"I hated it there," she continued, exhausted.

We suddenly found ourselves commiserating on the strange circumstances that had befallen us: the arrival of COVID-19, the school shutdowns, the fear and confusion that followed, our abysmal housing situations, and the everyday items that became biohazards overnight—the stores, the subways, the air, your average tabletops. The sun illuminated two dark circles around her eyes. *She's a college freshman*, I thought. How terrifying it must have been for her to be thrown into a pandemic-stricken strange new world—lonely, tired, frightened, without family or friends for help.

"I called and emailed and mailed letters to the Embassy for months," she sighed. "They finally let me on a flight in June. I missed that flight, though."

Might as well start over, people had told us. Getting on another flight would be close to impossible if you missed the first flight you were assigned on. I recalled my own seven-month wait with a shudder.

"At least I got on another flight," laughed Vân. The blinding sunlight swallowed her tiny, weary frame.

"I went to the ER in July. Called an Uber and dragged myself there," she muttered softly to the ground as though telling it her life story. She rose, long-suffering, exhausted.

"My body finally gave up on me," she sighed, a sad smile across her face.

I made the mistake of asking her if she had reached out for help.

"I wanted to," Bạch Vân snapped, eyes glowing with indignation. "I went to Zoom tutoring the other day, and the lady who was supposed to assign me a tutor kicked me out because she couldn't understand what I was saying." Her shoulders sagged. She hastily turned away to hide her tears. "I don't know how to tell people I *need help.* I'm scared they'll turn me away if they can't understand my English."

"Are you excited to be back?" I asked. Dragonflies fluttered in front of us. A group of quarantined travelers sprinted past us, laughing, talking, arms flailing. Yet the silence still clung to us, ominously, suffocatingly, even as the sound of conversation and laughter pierced the hot afternoon air.

"I don't know," she whispered, staring at a distance. "My parents are going through a divorce. Things aren't great at home either." She hung her head. Her shoulders felt heavy.

"I'm sorry I troubled you with all the details," she said softly. "Everyone here has been through so much."

"It's alright," I reassured her. We passed another puddle in silence.

"I'm never going back to Seattle again!" exclaimed Bạch Vân. The thick afternoon air stirred; more laughter rose from afar. "I'll probably have to return to finish college, but I won't go back there ever again after that. And I don't want to move cities or transfer schools, either. I'm scared of starting over."

She had nowhere to go, I told myself. The sun felt too hot, the sky too blue, the walk too exhausting.

She fidgeted. She fretted. She prodded at her phone and ran her hand through her hair as if her fingers had minds of their own.

"Oh well, at least we're home safe," she laughed, bitterly, forlornly.

Maybe, I thought, placing a hand on her shoulder. *Maybe it's going to be alright.*

3. Cô Vân.

"Do you know how to add that promotional code? The one the airline gave us for being on repatriation flights?" howled *cô* Vân. We were all trying to book flight tickets for the same town once quarantine ended. She poked her head out of the safety of her mosquito net. "Here, I'll show you," she said, frantically swatting swarming bugs as she barreled toward our bunks. Her teenagers had gone for an evening walk around the front lawn.

She squinted at my neighbor's phone. Darkness enveloped the quarantine camp; the last rays of sunlight had vanished behind the mountains. "Hurry up," she said, still swatting bugs, "so you all can get your flight tickets as soon as possible."

"Four more days," sighed the neighbor, peering at *cô* Vân. "Can't wait to get out of here."

"Don't test positive," laughed *cô* Vân. We all giggled. I caught a smile on her face, behind her mask.

Oh, to think that we hated each other only ten days ago.

She arrived with two teenagers and bulging boxes and bags in tow. Their bunks occupied the very far end of the room, away from foot traffic. We knew her as *cô* Vân ("Auntie Vân") or *cô ở cuối phòng* (literally "that auntie at the end of the room"). From a distance, she looked like every quarantined traveler in the room who laughed, sang, and mingled; up close, she was unapproachable and cold, conversing solely with the two teenagers in hushed tones and greeting passers-by with disinterested silence.

The teenagers. Her teenagers. We watched, exasperated, as *cô* Vân did everything for them: tidy their bunks, remind them to eat, hang up and take down their mosquito nets, and do their laundry; they, like her, rebuffed every friendly overture with quiet nonchalance. We observed in distaste as she scrambled to ensure they skipped lines for everything, even temperature checks, which everyone eventually had to be called up for. They, obnoxious, cold, and disinterested, irritated us. It was understandable that we left them alone. We knew better—or so we thought.

It all changed with the arrival of *nem*.

"Everyone gets two," I caught her muttering as she swiftly placed the oblong pieces of banana-leaf-wrapped pork onto each bunk. No one knew where they came from or how she got them here. Such delightful, delectable delicacies these were: savory, sweet, spicy, a party in your mouth! *Nem* brought us a welcoming respite from our monotonous diet of overcooked rice and bland fried eggs. *Nem* gave us a much-needed authentic taste of home. And for once, *nem* brought excitement to a roomful of long-suffering quarantined travelers. *Nem* reminded us dazed repatriation flight passengers that *we were finally home.*

In a sense, *nem* also brought *cô* Vân closer to us, and us to her.

"Any plans to return to the US?" interrupted the neighbor in the middle of *cô* Vân's promo-code tutorial. She curiously eyed *cô*, anticipating an answer. The response seemed obvious considering where we all came from. *Not now.*

"Pretty soon," said *cô* Vân. She didn't seem to mind the interruption. "I'll head back once the kids settle down with their parents."

Three pairs of eyes were on her. Our jaws dropped. *What is she talking about?*

"I'm a US citizen," she explained, looking up at us, bemused. "My family's in the US. I'm their aunt. Their parents sent them to the US for school, and they've been living with us since they were little. They keep calling me Mom though." A hint of pride lurked in her voice. She must have somehow spotted our hanging jaws in pitch darkness. *Good eye*, I thought.

"My son's going to college," said she, beaming with pride, "He's like their big brother."

"You're going to miss them," I remarked. Confusion still loomed. *Why is she bringing them back?*

"Their parents want them back because of COVID-19," she continued slowly, as if sensing our bewilderment. "I never wanted them to leave. But I thought, maybe it's safer for them here in Vietnam with their parents right now. I went with them on these flights because I'm worried about them flying by themselves. They've been through a lot, with all these lockdowns and school shutdowns going on."

"They're back!" she exclaimed, eyeing the two silhouettes shuffling through the front doorway. I found myself marveling at how quickly she could tell her niece and nephew's arrival. She rose from my neighbor's bunk. "Gotta help them put on their mosquito nets. Too many bugs here."

She made her way toward the two teenagers. We saw her smile at them and fumbled their mosquito nets, her hands trying to determine which string went where. We watched her do everything for them: sweep the floor, tidy their bunks, remind them to eat and exercise, make sure they receive the best possible food; we saw how she had stored everything on her bunk and left only a tiny patch for herself, just so there would be more space on the teenagers' bunks. We shuddered at her multi-flight trip: how she risked her health to make sure they returned home safely even as many of us had sworn off flying forever! We saw her quietly carrying the weight of her and the teenagers' fears and worries on her shoulders. It seemed as though she desperately wanted to protect them from this chaotic world. For her, nothing else mattered, neither her health nor safety, so long as her companions remained healthy and content.

For cô Vân, they'd always be her little kids.

Departures.

The test results came back negative.

How joyful it was as departure time neared! The women from the upstairs room hurriedly cleaned their bunks and packed their bags, laughing and chatting as they zipped, taped, locked, and weighed colorful suitcases and bulging boxes. Social media usernames, phone numbers, and promises to reconvene once COVID-19 was over were exchanged. Someone unveiled an out-of-tune guitar, and for once, travelers from all parts of Vietnam crowded the hallway, joining hands and singing an off-key version of Nối Vòng Tay Lớn, a Vietnamese song about unity and friendship.

Whose idea was it to pick this song, I marveled. How well-thought-out the song choice was.

Dawn. Downstairs, a cargo truck idled. The camp was alive with no-longer-quarantined travelers loading their belongings onto the truck to be taken to the airport. I tossed Bạch Vân's nearly-forgotten suitcase on the truck before she left it behind; I saw *cô* Vân count her suitcases and boxes before throwing them aboard. I recalled *cô*, my airplane seatmate, and wondered if anyone had helped her with her bags. Amidst the crowd of people excitedly manhandling their luggage, I pictured others I had met during our journey home—my remaining roommates, the folks from neighboring rooms, the people on our flights—carrying months' worth of fears, worries, struggles, ruined plans, stories, and their own versions of America and the American Dream buried under heavy boxes and bags and hidden behind face masks. I saw myself in them—for I, too, was a quarantined traveler bringing home my own stories, struggles, and fears. I watched them unable to articulate their pain in both Vietnamese and English. I wanted to hug them, listen to all of their stories, and retell their struggles, but it was too late. They left hours ago, and only a handful of us remained, waiting for the last bus of the day to the airport.

My heart ached. *What has COVID-19 done? I wanted to scream. How many people are sick? How many have lost their lives? How many more people are still separated from their loved ones?* Yet the melody of my roommates' laughter and the mangled version of *Nối Vòng Tay Lớn* lingered. It was the laughter, the bad singing, the resilience, the thoughts of home, the hopes for a better future—all that made us human—that gave us the will to carry on. We humans are fragile, fallible, and long-suffering, but even as COVID-19 ravages, it is our own fragility and spirit that allows us to prevail.

Farewell, I said to my fellow travelers as we parted, *and may we meet again at a better time.*

Honorable Mention—Creative Nonfiction

Muntaha Haq

Things Unseen

I am a Muslim girl who lives in the perfect neighborhood, guarded by a white picket fence and suburban ideals. My parents raised me to be a respectable young woman, smiling but never with teeth. I do well in school, besides the occasional math test, and I have enough friends to keep me company. I am a Muslim girl living in the perfect neighborhood and I have a secret.

I don't believe in God.

I believe in the feeling of hot pavement on my bare feet, the noisy chatter of cicadas, the push and pull of ocean tides—I believe in what I can see. When my back is pressed against the bathroom door, this is what I tell myself. But then there are times, few and far in between, I believe in something far greater.

• • •

In the second grade, my best friend and I had an argument. I remember burying my face into a pillow, tears blurring my vision. That night, I sat on my bed with my hands cupped together. At eight years old, I have yet to learn the universal truth about being eight years old: fights end as easily as they begin. *Allah, I need her in my life*, I pray.

The next day, she tackles me into a hug before I can even walk through the door. The smile on my face is so big, it practically splits open. *Is this the power of God*? I didn't realize it then, but that would be the last time I believed someone would answer my prayers.

• • •

In a diner, somewhere between Virginia and Tennessee, the coffee grows cold. I cut into a thick stack of pancakes, scraping off whipped cream and slathering maple syrup in its place. Only two more hours until I see my sister again, now a proud student at the University of Tennessee.

Loud voices interrupt my thoughts: my parents are fighting. I frown, aggressively digging my fork into a platter of hash browns. *Are they seriously arguing about whether or not to order bread?*

Abu stands up and slams his fist on the table, loud enough to rattle the silverware. The entire diner is stunned silent, and I can barely make out the whistling of a tea kettle. The air is stifling with tension, a toddler a few seats over begins to cry.

My eyes widen, they're no longer arguing, they're screaming. I sit frozen in my seat, ducking my head in embarrassment. The diner is filled with the harsh sounds of a foreign language, and I pray to Allah that my parents remember their place.

Abu storms out of the diner, leaving the half-eaten breakfast platter, his wife, and his daughter behind. I run after him.

Four hours later, the episode at the diner is the least of my concern. Abu lays in a hotel bed, his eyes glazed over and his skin hot to the touch. Every time I bring soup to his mouth, it dribbles from the side of his lips. I've never seen Abu so defenseless, so vulnerable.

There is no amount of time that can erase that image of my father.

Ma is shouting, lashing like a wild animal. She calls Abu names worse than the ones from before, but there's no heat behind her words. There's fear. Ma is terrified because right now, she's as useless as I am.

That night, I pray to Allah, cupping my hands as if I were a child. I pray not out of want but out of need. I am sixteen years old, and I refuse to lose my father, it's too soon.

In two days, Abu is fine to drive. We leave Knoxville, the three of us, with a bitter taste in our mouths. I hum my prayers and ignore the empty aching in my chest. Every so often, I am reminded of how small I am. Insignificant. Fleeting. And in those moments, there is nothing to do but believe. Shut your eyes, clench your fists, and believe as hard as you can. Who is more devout a worshipper than he who begs on his knees? I thank Allah that it is three passengers in our car and not two.

• • •

My friend parks her car in my driveway, the clock reads 12:16. I am eighteen years old, and the minute Ma sees my face, I will remain eighteen. Infinitely.

We sit in silence, because despite the ticking clock, we both know what lies beyond those doors. My parents have always been strict with me: my clothes, my grades, my words. I rarely go out as it is, but the few times I do, I'm expected to come home exactly when I promise. And yet here I am, coming home past midnight like an "American" girl.

I hear myself talking, rambling really, desperate to stay beside my friend. I tell her that nowadays, my house is quiet. Part of me thinks it's been that way ever since my sister left for college three years ago. When I'm home, just Abu, Ma, and I, the quiet suffocates me. My only comfort is the droning static of our TV, running headlines no one cares to remember. I've gotten used to walking on eggshells, worried that if I speak loud enough, I'll break the fragile silence.

When I look over, my friend is crying. We cry because we're teenage girls and this is what teenage girls do. They cry and hug each other and wonder when it was they stopped being children. I had a crappy day at school, and all I wanted was to have a milkshake and fries with my friends. One hour of laughter turned into two, which turned into three—I never meant to stay out past midnight. I hug her one last time and take a deep breath.

Hell awaits me.

When my friend picks me up for rehearsal the next morning, the world seems pale. If either of us is surprised that I'm sitting in her car at all, we don't say.

During a lapse in the conversation, her lips tug into a slight smile. Last night, my friend told her mother about me. She was crying and her mother held her close in her arms and they prayed.

For me.

Something inside me splinters, cracks. Because at eighteen years old, my heart is not the same as it was in the second grade. I had become a brittle, hollow shell of my former self. And again, I begin to cry. I'm crying because I want to believe in the God that unites mothers and daughters, the God that is kind. But why is it when I close my eyes, the God I see is the one who abandoned me? Something changed between now and then, I had lost my way. I forgot how it felt to rely on others, be vulnerable.

I hug my friend once we reach a stoplight. I'm angry with myself because it hurts to breathe, but I've never heard words so tender. Like a salve, healing cuts old and new, the ones I never knew I had to begin with.

⋯

Today, my world is not so simple. I believe in what I can see, but maybe I believe in things unseen too. I believe in the feeling of hot pavement on my bare feet, the noisy chatter of cicadas, the push and pull of ocean tides, but now I also believe in something much greater. I realized that while growing up, I had lost faith, not in Allah, but in the people I love most. At eight years old, having faith in your friends and family is second nature. It comes as easily as breathing. At eighteen, having faith in anyone or anything is a constant battle.

At eighteen and three quarters, I have learned important lessons—namely to never allow fear to overcome love. My most intimate memories of worship are not on the floors of a mosque, nor church, nor synagogue—they are memories with my friends and family. Their mercy, their strength, their unity inspires me. I've come to believe that the beauty of God is best reflected in his humble creation: man. I am a Muslim girl living in the perfect neighborhood and I have a secret—I am learning to trust again.

First Place—Fiction

Sanjana Ramanathan
The Lady of the Butterflies

The slow heat of summer was just beginning to roll in when the Lady arrived in Kittery.

Our town was small so everyone, especially us kids, noticed when the low cabin in the middle of the woods—the one that was *supposed* to be abandoned—was suddenly occupied. Occupied by a woman, old but not yet wrinkled, with eyes that cut us like knives when we tried to peer in through her windows.

For weeks we skirted the woodland around her house, dragging our bikes through the dirt as we speculated in hushed voices.

"She's probably some sort of criminal," My older brother, Jacob, said. "And that cabin is her safehouse. She's probably murdered at least fifteen people!"

"Maybe she's a secret agent from Russia," I ventured. "Maybe this is her base, and she's spying on the government."

The other kids laughed at that. Jacob looped an arm around my neck and rubbed his knuckles against my head, saying, "If she were a spy, she wouldn't have come to Kittery. This is the middle of nowhere."

I flushed, ducking out of his grasp. "She looks Russian."

"She's probably a witch," Malcolm said. Malcolm was big but quiet, so when he talked, people listened. "I think she knows magic."

All of us, even Jacob, nodded. And because Malcolm had said it, it became true: The Lady of the woods was a witch.

The summer dragged on as we spent our days as kids did, languid yet restless. One day, someone dared Jenny to knock on the witch's door. We all watched, ducked behind the drooping juniper, as she rapped twice on the wood.

The door opened, and Jenny disappeared inside.

The shadows stretched as we waited with bated breath. Our whispers carried on even as the sun dipped low and our curfews loomed closer. Surely if Jenny were in trouble, we would have heard *something*?

Then she emerged, beaming. As she skipped toward us, a little blue butterfly hovered around her right ear.

Jenny said, smiling, "She can do magic! She can!"

We all crowded around her, begging her to share. Jenny told us that the Lady didn't like being called a witch, but she had one special trick. She could take a memory, whatever memory you wanted, and turn it into a butterfly.

We all looked at the butterfly, now seated on Jenny's shoulder. It flapped its brilliant blue wings.

"So that thing is a memory?" Jacob asked, reaching out to prod the butterfly carefully. It shuddered under his touch but stayed on Jenny's shoulder. It must have been magical; any *real* butterfly would have flown away by now.

"The Lady said when I'm ready, I can have the memory back. But until then, it will stay outside my head, like this," said Jenny.

"What's the memory?" asked little Ben, his eyes round as saucers.

"I dunno," Jenny shrugged. "I just remember it was something embarrassing."

We all looked at each other, stunned. *Real* magic. It seemed impossible.

I tried to think of something I wanted to forget, but nothing came to mind. We were just kids. I looked at Malcolm, whose eyes were latched onto the beautiful butterfly. His father had drowned last year in a boating accident. Maybe he wanted to forget the funeral, or maybe it was the good memories that hurt more.

During the rest of the summer, the other kids eventually made their way into the cabin and came out with a little butterfly hovering around their head. The colors, shapes, and sizes of the butterflies varied, but they always stayed next to their person, never straying. The day Jacob went in, I wanted to follow him. What did he want to forget? Was it the time I spilled ice cream on him in front of Clara at the fair, just before he had planned to ask her out? Was it when he broke his bike and Dad yelled at him so hard, he started crying on the street?

When Jacob came out, his butterfly was brown-flecked white. "You should try it," he told me. "I don't know how to describe it, but I feel really free."

But I didn't want to. I was scared, suddenly. Scared of my friends. Scared of the way Jacob was inexplicably mature, the way Jenny was bubbly and Clara was confident. Scared of the way Malcolm was distantly serene, like someone had pushed cotton behind his eyes and now his brain was full of fuzz. He still talked the same but he *wasn't* the same, and I was scared of the way just taking a memory away could change a person so much.

By the end of the summer, everyone had a butterfly but me. We met up by the lake, our bike tires dragging through the slick mud. We all looked around at each other.

"I think it's time," said Malcolm. For the first time since his orange butterfly had appeared, he sounded truly sad.

The others nodded, though I didn't understand. One by one, they sat down in the dirt and opened their mouths. The butterflies, as if waiting for the cue, crawled in. I watched them, flapping their wings as they wriggled down my friends' throats. I gagged.

And one by one, I saw my friends change—or rather, unchange. Become themselves again. Jenny's aloofness, Clara's shyness, little Ben's curiosity, Jacob's familiar scowl. The sadness in Malcolm's eyes was back, too; I hated that I was happy to see it.

· · ·

Years passed, and most of us left Kittery behind. It was a tiny town, without much room for anyone with dreams bigger than owning a fishing boat. We stretched our limbs and stretched out across the country, losing touch. I hadn't spoken to anyone but Jacob in years.

The Lady of the woods became a bedtime story I told my daughter, Ruby. She took it as seriously as she took the Tooth Fairy or Santa Claus, which is to say not at all. She was always a precocious child. When I told her the story of my friends and their beautiful butterflies, she laughed like windchimes, and it was easy to think it was all just make-believe.

When I lost Ruby, the worst part was how senseless it was. A car accident; the other driver was drunk. Logically, I knew there was nothing I could have done. But my heart just thumped with fury, with agony, with memories.

Years and years after that fateful summer, I still remembered the serenity in Malcolm's eyes. I couldn't stop thinking of the woman, the witch, who was able to turn his pain into something so beautiful. The possibility of her taking Ruby away was both unbearable and tantalizing. The thought was incessantly in my mind.

For the first time in years, I returned to Kittery. It was almost on autopilot; I didn't want to think because thinking became remembering became grieving. All I wanted now was to forget.

Even now, I knew the way through the woods well. I stomped through the ivy, ignoring the way that the brambles tore through my clothes. The cabin was the same as I remembered it, and I knocked twice on the door. *Thump, thump.*

The door opened, and there she was. She hadn't changed since my childhood, but somehow that didn't surprise me.

"You are here for help," she said, her voice soft. Her accent was unfamiliar (*not Russian, I thought, near hysterically*) but somehow soothing.

"Yes," I told her. "I need help. I need you to take away a memory."

She led me inside, gesturing for me to sit in a chair at the nearby kitchen table. Her furniture was humble, cozy even. Not what my childhood imagination had pictured a witch's house would look like. "I can do that. I can turn your memory into something easier to handle, until you're ready to face it again."

"How will I know when I'm ready?"

She gave me a look with her sharp-dark eyes. "You will know."

"What if I'm never ready?"

She made a gesture that was almost a shrug. "Then you will know that, too."

I leaned back in the chair, sucking in a breath. I thought of Ruby and her bright smile, the smile I would never see again; my heart mourned in response. Relief was so, so close, and yet—

The Lady leaned in close. "What is the memory?"

Ruby's laugh rang in my ears.

"My memory of you."

She drew back, her brow furrowed. "Of me?"

"Yes," I closed my eyes. "As long as I know you're here, I'll be tempted to make things easier." I thought of Ruby's bright eyes, blinking up at me, and my chest ached. "I don't want easy."

• • •

I stumbled through the woods, dizzy. I couldn't remember how I had ended up back in Kittery. Perhaps I had come out here to find some peace after Ruby's death. Yes, that seemed right.

Something feather-light brushed past my ear—a wing. I reached up and a butterfly, black and red, rested on my hand.

Instinctively, I knew exactly what this creature was, although I didn't know how. It was a memory. *My* memory. I didn't know of what; all I knew was that it was dangerous.

I curled my fingers over it, crushing its body against my palm. I felt it struggle, thin wings tearing, until it was finally, mercifully still.

Second Place—Fiction

Muntaha Haq
Green Melon Bars

The air in Chinatown is an oppressive and sweltering heat, capable of slowing time itself. Everyone curses the sun, willing its proud heart to stop beating. Children begin to cry out to their mothers, begging for shaved ice. Grannies sit under the shade and fold magazines into delicate paper fans. Vendors sell frozen water bottles, yelling until their voices grow hoarse. Even in the summer heat, the market is alive with chaos.

Jun marches toward the convenience store, silently reciting her grocery list. Every step feels as if she's resisting air, resisting gravity, and she wonders if this is how astronauts feel. She decides that if it is, she's wasted too much time dreaming about space. When Jun finally walks through the sliding doors, she sighs in relief.

"Hey, Mr. Choi!" Jun smiles at the older man at the counter, who offers a curt nod in response. She rolls her eyes, watching as Mr. Choi argues with a customer.

Jun grabs a few bricks of instant ramen before stopping at the ice cream freezer. She opens the door and lets the cold air out. A happy noise escapes her throat, she could stay here forever.

"Get some ice cream and close it," Mr. Choi barks. The old man lifts his head from his newspaper, glaring at Jun from across the aisle. Without turning around, she waves him off. Jun frowns, eyes darting between the different flavors. Oolong, red bean paste, where are the melon bars?

"Mr. Choi, you're out of stock," Jun says, closing the freezer door. The other flavors are tasty enough, but melon ice cream is *perfect* for the summer. Jun hears Mr. Choi close his newspaper, muttering curses under his breath.

"What is it now, Jun?" Mr. Choi says, running a hand over his face. He peers into the freezer, lifting the different boxes of popsicles.

"You're out of green melon," Jun yawns, stretching her arms. She props the freezer door open with her hip to keep it from hitting Mr. Choi.

"Oh, those aren't coming back," Mr. Choi says, shrugging, "low demand, I think." He hands her a matcha popsicle and ruffles her hair.

Jun's mouth opens, and she's left holding the popsicle in her hand. The melon ice creams were always here, always on the bottom rack of the freezer. How could they just be *gone*? Jun grabs Mr. Choi's arm to keep him from leaving. His eyes widen as he tries to pull from her grasp, but Jun's hand stays firm.

"What do you mean they're not coming back? Order some more." Jun says, her voice rising.

Mr. Choi shakes his head, "They're not shipping to the East coast, I can't just 'order more.'" Jun feels her throat close, tears beginning to brim her eyes. She coughs, wiping her eyes with the back of her hand.

"I don't want this," Jun says, shoving the popsicle into Mr. Choi's chest. Mr. Choi frowns, staring at Jun with confused eyes. Her cheeks begin to flush red, finally processing the scene she created. Jun runs out of the store, having completely forgotten her groceries. Mr. Choi yells after her.

"You're late, I sent you for groceries an hour," Ru says, leaning over the kitchen counter. Jun reaches for a water bottle, pressing it against her warm forehead.

"Yeah, yeah, sorry, I forgot about those," Jun says, propping herself on the counter.

"You forgot the groceries? Jun, seriously we—"

"Can you shut up for like two seconds? They're just groceries!" She says, throwing her arms in the air. Jun bites the inside of her cheek, willing herself not to cry. She has no idea why she even yelled in the first place. Jun prays Mr. Choi is in a forgiving mood, she feels embarrassed for grabbing him like that. She was being silly; they were just ice cream bars after all.

But they weren't. When she was younger, Jun hated shopping in Chinatown, so Ma always promised Jun a popsicle. Ma always bought Jun and Ru the melon flavor and the three of them would enjoy it on the grass. There was nothing better than the sweet, melon flavored ice cream on a summer day. It wasn't just popsicles; it was their *childhood*. Surely Ru would feel the same way?

"Are you okay?" Ru sits atop the counter, worry in his voice.

Jun inhales, if anyone could understand, it would be Ru. He is quiet and serious and not at all like Jun, but he was her brother. Even when she spoke in bursts of emotion, she could count on Ru to understand. Right?

"Jun, you're going to have to apologize to Mr. Choi," Ru says, once she finishes explaining. He rubs his temples, as if Jun was causing a headache.

"That's what you got from all this?"

"What I 'got from this' is you practically assaulted our family friend."

"Jesus, I'll apologize!" Jun yells, ignoring the hitch in her voice. Of course, Ru didn't understand, how could he?

Jun wakes up to the smell of dumplings. She shakes her head; it can't be dumplings. Ru is even worse a cook than she is, which is somewhat of an accomplishment. She wipes the sleep from her eyes, entering the kitchen yawning.

Her eyes widen, Ru is standing over the bamboo steamer. Could he actually be making dumplings? Jun can't help but smile, she can smell the pork and cabbage and bok choy—it's delicious.

"Hey," Ru says, awkwardly waving a hand.

"Hi."

"You know it's okay to miss Ma, right?" Ru bursts out. Jun's eyes widen in shock, her brother never mentioned Ma unless she did. Jun watches him, the way his hands anxiously toy with a pair of chopsticks.

She sighs, bringing soy sauce out of the fridge to start a dipping sauce. "What're you talking about?" She stirs soy sauce and water into a bowl, streaming in drops of sesame oil.

"It's really hard having Ma in China, but she's going to come back as soon as Grandma's better," Ru continues, taking dishes out of the pantry.

Jun blinks away her tears, biting her lip to keep from talking. They work in silence, Jun crushing red pepper for the dipping sauce and Ru taking the dumplings off the parchment paper. She clears her throat, "Of course I do, she'll be back in no time."

Ru finally lifts his head from the steamer and smiles, "Good. In the meantime, these might help. They're not popsicles, but they're something."

He slides her a plate of dumplings, watching her expectantly. Jun prods at a dumpling with a chopstick, she can already tell that the skin is too thick and doughy. Ru is still watching her from the corner of his eyes when she finally takes a bite. She blows steam to keep her tongue from burning, but the flavor is nice. The pork is garlicy and gingery and tastes as it should.

"But?" Ru asks, taking a bite of a dumpling himself.

Jun laughs as he begins fanning his mouth, he was never much good at spicy foods. "You over seasoned," she says, smiling, "but these aren't half bad."

Honorable Mention—Fiction

Mikayla Butz-Weidner
The Tragedy of Mr. and Mrs. Timothy Beckett

    Looking back upon my extensive career, I've come to know the ins and outs of disaster. I've seen some of the most sinister, the most gnarled, the dastardly unthinkable. You see, I've been here and there. After the war, I moved across the pond from my native Sutton where I found myself just outside Boston, in Medford, to be precise. Equally heinous were the cases in Medford as they were in London, but in both spots found the most gruesome crimes to be amongst the domestics. In studying the man and wife, you come to know them as intimately as they know each other, knowing what they like, what they hate, the faults in their characters, the crinkles in their noses and lines in their foreheads, the way their minds work. My brother died in the trenches, and mother didn't last much longer after that, so I've been on my own all these years, just me and Mr. Thomas, my Himalayan cat. It's really enough, but I do find myself feeling attached to some of these people I've invested my days in studying. Reading files, visiting their homes, piecing their stories together, I've come to consider them friends, nearly. I've met them at their ends, but they speak so much that I can see the rest for myself.

    Mr. Timothy Beckett was a precocious man of forty. He wore a brown suit most days and said he liked to waltz, though he probably preferred a foxtrot. He met his wife, Miss Melinda Bates, in their more youthful days, when she was a Radcliffe girl and he a Harvard boy (though she dropped out after three years, in time for the wedding). Her chestnut brown hair against her crimson fisherman sweater caught his eyes at the library, and from there it was laughs on the quad and tip-toes into each other's dormitories past curfew. Though she beat him out in wit and pedigree, his tweed jackets and smell of cigars reminded her of her father, and so she held her tongue while they fell in love. They met in November, he graduated in April, and they were married that June.

    As it so often goes, suburban life grew tiresome on their marriage. Their nights out in the North End grew fewer and more seldom. Friends from university married and moved away—such is life—and soon, it was just the Becketts in their cozy Italianate, the only one on a block of colonials. Mr. Beckett had admired her rabble-rouser ways when they'd met—thinking of the girl who'd argue with professors and hide cigarettes in her garter, the girl who'd hike up her skirt and climb the tree and crawl through his dormitory window at night—but watching her put on lipstick for church services each Sunday turned his old image of her to a faint memory, and he wondered if it had ever really been true. Likewise, the novelty of his cufflinks and handkerchiefs ceased to impress her, and she wished she hadn't locked herself down at the first sight of familiarity. Nonetheless, they continued to act happy with one another. They ate dinner together, went to the pictures a couple times a month, and made love on the special occasions. I believe it was the hankering for more that got to them. If they'd gotten a place in Beacon Hill over Medford, the whole mess could have been avoided.

All the neighbors guessed that the Becketts were as happy as any couple could be, doting on their porch and garden. Between the Becketts themselves though, their quiet resentment boiled within them and soon turned to hate. I've often found that a man can come to know his wife so well that she becomes a metaphor for all he wishes to escape from, and vice versa, and so on.

It, the rot, that is, started with Mrs. Beckett, née Bates. She knew her good name wouldn't withstand a divorce, and she didn't have it in her New England heart to tell Mr. Beckett that his cigars bothered her, that his green argyle was worn and tired, that she no longer loved him as she once did. Deep down, she wished for a car accident, but as he walked to work each day, she knew it was a hopeless dream.

And so, instead, she grew increasingly taciturn. Each night, dinner was over much faster than usual, his banal comments were met with far fewer quips, and they were in bed with the lights out early enough that the boisterous laughs of their neighbors across the street kept them up. They started shuttering the windows at night. Mr. Beckett interpreted his wife's sudden reserve to be her pride showing, as if it were a judgement of his worth as a man, and her sparing words were ratings of her fleeting affection. You see, he wasn't of low birth, but he was lower than her, and he could never forget it, even if the room was silent. Raising the question would spark a conversation, one he had spent their entire courtship avoiding, one he didn't have in him to weather.

Their etiquette and charm only fastened their resolution to the very marriage they loathed. Though they wished little harm on one another, widow and widower were their respective aspirations; all they had to do was pick their poison. Both people true to their words, they both selected the ever-literal poison, arsenic, of course.

Since the first Monday they returned from their honeymoon, the third Tuesday of each month had always been steak night. In my investigation, I found their marriage to be riddled with these kinds of strictures, as if reaching for some semblance of a happy living for others to recognize. Though not so devoted to each other, they were earnestly dedicated to the show of it all and what people would think.

She knew he had a weakness for sugar in his afternoon tea, and he knew she had a weakness for salt on her dinner, no matter the meal. Dinner was at six, but tea was at four. Both being totally blind to the other's plot, they carried on with their day as if it were any other steak night. In my investigation, it became clear that Mr. and Mrs. were likely sold the arsenic by the same man, for Medford, as we on the force see it, is a bit of an arsenic desert. He was the only man on Earth who could have done anything to stop them. Instead, he sealed and sold their fates.

She swapped the sugar for arsenic while he was at the bank, and he snuck arsenic into the salt shaker while she put on the kettle for his tea. Mr. Timothy Beckett was dead by a quarter to five, and the widow Mrs. Beckett's steak was done at half past. His body lay cold in the drawing room as her head fell to the table, knocking over her wine, and landing right on her dinner for one.

They weren't found until the following night, when their neighbors, the Emerson's, came over for Tuesday bridge, which the late Mr. Beckett had rescheduled earlier in the week for Wednesday because "something had come up."

As a precaution, and I'll admit it, a nicety—as I see little time off the bench these days compared to some of the younger cats on the force—I was called to the scene that night. It seemed like some kind of accident, water contamination or gas leak, and I was ready to dismiss it as another housewife's cooking error, but in walking through the kitchen, I saw posted on the refrigerator was a grocery list, penned in handwriting that matched Mrs. Beckett's checks, and on it read "1 steak." With a cursory or novice look, this may not stand out, but there I thought, *why would a wife cooking for two be buying for one?* At that moment, my confidence restored, I called it, with reason to think this was no accident, but really, two coinciding—colliding, rather—acts of domestic homicide. She was certainly a minx, but her sense of propriety and knack for planning brought her posthumous conviction. Mr. Beckett, on the other hand, was a buffoon in his delivery, and left dashes of arsenic all around the salt shaker and the remainder of the substance in his coat pocket.

I attended their funeral the following week, before any verdict had been made public. For a marriage as prolonged and as dedicated to the show of bliss as the Becketts', their empty service was the tragedy of it all. Two, maybe three, benches were full at most. I sat in the back. That family name Melinda long suffered to protect failed to show any of its faces. The Emersons, those loyal bridge friends, sat up front, Mrs. Emerson weeping and Mr. offering his handkerchief.

As per a stipulation for her family's blessing on the eve of her engagement, Mr. and Mrs. Beckett were buried side by side in the Bates family plot. "Till death do us part" had given them a sense of hope, but their marital pursuit to appear picturesque bound them in love in the eyes of their friends, and thus, despite having taken such deliberate steps to rid themselves of the other, they lie together eternally.

First Place—Humor

Tim Hanlon

A Letter to Tony

Dear Dr. Anthony Stephen Fauci,

Listen, I know you're out here doing your best to get rid of me and, honestly, I don't blame you. You were probably all set to retire with no intentions of ever making your position so politicized or public. Now, day after day, you have to constantly deal with my antics. Four years ago, you and I had never met—now we are each other's greatest adversaries. I have to hand it to you, doctor, you have put up an excellent fight, but I'm truly not going anywhere soon.

Tony (if I may) you're a smart, sensible guy, but do you really think these lunatics are going to allow you to vaccinate against me? After all, we all know that in order for the FDA to approve a vaccine it absolutely *has* to include a microchip so they can one day control your every move.[1] You and I both know that the first ones to complain about this are the ones who impulsively check "Agree to Terms and Agreements" on their new government tracker—I think you humans call them iPhones?—every year. They're also the first to post *"Leaving for a 10-day Mexican Cruise with the whole family. These margaritas better be as authentic as the ones from the Mexican Tavern in rural Idaho xoxo. This is much needed!"* on their public Facebook page with a picture of her and her partner wearing sombreros and ponchos—even though they aren't racist, and this clearly isn't cultural appropriation. Let's be honest though, what we all really read is *"No one will be home for 10 days and we probably didn't even bother to remove the key from under the front door mat or off the grill on the back deck. Feel free to take all our things, and we will be so devastated and confused as to how anyone knew we weren't home."*

But hey, I guess that is Orange's America for you, Tony baby. If these people ever put their face into a book, you'd finally be able to retire, and I'd be squashed like the current global economy. Who knows, maybe you and I would even be sharing drinks on a nice tropical vacation with our families. Did you know the husband and I are up to six strains now? We will have to get together soon so you can meet the whole crew.

Now I really hesitate to compare myself to such an icon and model of the ever so wonderful system of capitalism, but I really think I am turning into the modern-day Amazon.[2] They have same day shipping; I have same day infection. Amazon does business across the world; I have traveled the world. They make billions of dollars; I have cost billions of dollars. They have infiltrated your computer's algorithms; I have infiltrated your body's immune system. In the end, Jeff Bezos and I aren't that different: neither of us have any hair, we aren't loyal to just one woman, and we both control more land than the British Empire ever did. In some regards, though, I like to think I am even better than Amazon. I take over existing hospitals instead of building new and massive warehouses

---

1 To be clear, this is a satire and microchips are not put in vaccines. That is what Starbucks coffee is for.
2 It's amazing how with all the talk about me, you all aren't getting targeted ads selling me.

that demolish hundreds of homes in low-income neighborhoods. Hell, I hardly take up any space at all. You can't even see me, but everywhere you look there's an Amazon building, vehicle, package, or aircraft. I also don't make creepy commercials with your holiday packages singing to you. Best of all, no one has to pay to order me. You just get me for free.[3]

Although, Tony, we can't forget small businesses (well, actually, it seems like we can). I will be helping the small business industry through Pfizer/BioNTech's new vaccine. Just think of all the hundreds of millions of dollars I will make them. I know big pharma is a struggling industry and is the model for how not to price gouge, so it will be nice to help such a charitable cause grow. Who knows, maybe the CEOs of these companies will finally be able to afford their fourth jet for their 9-year-old's Christmas gift. Do you think you could suggest a government stimulus package for these poor people? Just a small loan of a million dollars should do the trick. As a man of science, you must appreciate that the suggestion for a million dollars is based on the everlasting and prosperous success of our lord and savior Donald J. Trump and his similar loan from his daddy dearest.

Tony, I have been in a hospital or two, you know just doing, umm how you say "volunteer work" for the Russian government,[4] and the only true pandemic I can see is that absolute mess you call hospital food. Honestly, the doctors and nurses might be trying to get you out of there but the food sure as hell isn't. You go in for a simple broken finger and you leave needing a double full body transplant after eating the crackers alone. Speaking of questionable cafeteria food, have you been to an American public school lately?

This is truly exhausting. The Americans are making this entirely too easy for me and I just need a goddamn break. Like come on. You have these people out there yelling "All lives matter." Clearly, they don't believe so because many of the same ones are also saying "I will not put on a mask to protect my life and other lives." Don't get me wrong, these people are great for business—the Rona family could not be happier—but you should really talk with your counterpart Betsy DeVos about continuing to defund public schools because it is clearly making my life way too easy.[5]

Listen, I know it's hard for you all. You can see me just as well as Manti Teo's girlfriend, John Cena, and God.[6] But, as Liam Neeson so elegantly stated in the cult classic movie *Taken:* "I will not look for you, I will not pursue you. But if you don't [wear a mask and social distance], I will look for you, I will find you, and I will kill you."

---

3   Unless, of course, you are on one of the American health insurance plans. Then you'll have to take out a third mortgage, win the $1.4 billion lottery, and sacrifice your first born before you can even think about using the pen to fill out your intake forms. Don't get me started on how to cover your medical bills.
4   For legal reasons, due to my ever so obvious contract with the KGB, this is entirely a joke and I have no relation to Russian spies, the 2016 election results, or why Long John Silver's is still in business.
5   Granted, by the time you are reading this Betsy is likely long gone and she's out sailing the seas to search for her lost yacht. Yet another sheepishly deprived and underprivileged soul. Gone too soon but never forgotten by the students she underfunded and forced back into the ever so prosperous poverty loop.
6   Although, it does seem like those who would absolutely die for God would also die from me because religion is their one true mask.

Nevertheless, I digress. This is a long-winded way of me saying we are planning to bring the pumpkin pie to the New Year's party, so let us know if any of the Faucis have any food allergies.

With all the love,

Covid

xoxo

Second Place—Humor

Max Gallagher

Dog-Walking 101

(*a comprehensive, seven-step guide to taking your furry friend into the great unknown.**)

*Exercise caution before beginning your journey through these seven steps.

STEP ONE: Find a dog.

    This may seem obvious to you, and if that's the case, I applaud your intuition. However, you must remember that you are gifted in ways most of us are not. You'll need to be patient while the rest of the world catches up.

    To find a dog, you must know where to look. Conveniently, dogs can be found almost anywhere! Easy places to check include but are not limited to:

a pet adoption store,

a reputable breeder,

a cousin's house,

a beach landscape,

a pretty painting,

an old photograph (hidden at the bottom of a drawer and that you weren't meant to find),

a memory,

a dream,

a wish,

a hope,

alone (and so cold, so very cold, and so very alone),

the farmer's market,

etcetera.

    Like I said, almost anywhere! It may be useful to note from where you obtain your dog, for they are affected by their specific locationality, as we all are. We are products of our time and our space—if your dog comes from a stinky time or place, you may never be able to wash away the funk.

STEP TWO: Call that dog your own.

    Included in this step could be a great many sub-steps, like naming the dog! And inviting the dog into your home (and I hope that you do have a home (a (warm) place to call your own))! Or buying a dog bed for the dog, and hand stitching their given name onto the front of the dog bed (even though you know they can't read, but wouldn't they just love it if they could read?) Plus, you can read it, and you like it!

I'm only hinting at sub-steps, for the act of possession is an intensely personal one. You are free to complete this step as you see fit, so long as you remember that what you are possessing is not an object; it is another living thing. An animal. A baby! And it barks, when there's something to be said! And it squints, when there's something to be seen! And it snores, when there are dreams to be had. With this in mind, possess with care. We become that which possesses us. Just as we become our possessions. Just as we have always been ourselves.

STEP THREE: Put that dog on a leash!

Read this step again (silently, in your head). And now read it one more time (aloud, as a disgruntled old woman). And now just once more, please (aloud, as a cartoon duck). This is the same duck which has haunted your nightmares since childhood—you went to Disneyland and that same cartoon duck took off its large plush head and you saw a human man underneath (and that man smiled at you with far too many teeth)and then he sneezed in your hair. Remember the way it feels to read these words. Remember the way it feels to hear these words (again). Remember these words.

Of course, implied in this step are all the *traditional sub-steps of capitalism*: you save up your money for a leash, you dream long and hard that, someday, you could become the kind of person (a good person) who owns a dog leash—but eventually you burn all your savings on something that is not a leash (on a video game (Mario Kart, to be specific, your favorite game as a child)), and you feel sad about how selfish you've been. And in your sadness, you neglect to play your new video game. You would have played as Toad, because you're *always* Toad (for some reason)—so you sell back your recent indulgence (to your local Best Buy)—you are refunded a negligible amount of cash—and you start over again from the top.

You know—all the normal, traditional, sub-steps.

Optionally, once you do obtain a leash, you may choose to hand stitch your dog's given name onto the leash. I've found a simple backstitch to be effective in the majority of leashes—and dogs really just seem to love it!

STEP FOUR: Walk outside with your leashed dog.

This step might seem simple, but it's really rather complex when you think about it, but you didn't think about it, did you? Of course, you didn't think about it, because you do not think (that's what I'm here for).

To step outside of your home implies an acceptance that you may never return to your home. In the same way, going to sleep every night implies an acceptance that you may never again wake up. Eating implies acceptance of hunger. Breathing implies acceptance of breathlessness (joyous breathlessness in the middle of the night, when the moon couldn't possibly shine brighter, and you can see, even if only for a moment, the oneness of all things, and then the moon somehow does shine brighter) and you hope for this night to be endless, and you remember to breathe, if only to continue being here and forever and alive). Living implies acceptance that life will end, for death is simply the other part of life.

Of course, acceptance is only the implication of being. It takes a great deal of bravery to accept wholly, without implication. It takes a great deal of bravery to go on stepping (into the outdoors and into the unknown) without fear.

STEP FIVE: Greet whoever you may meet while outside.

Suppose, if only just for an instant, that you are outside (which means in this instant you are brave), and you see an old man sitting on his porch, and near this old man on his porch you see, staked into a proudly green lawn, a sign for a politician (one for whom you did not vote, for whom you would never vote, and for whom you hold a passionate distaste).

Imagine this man, sitting on his porch, with the political sign on his lawn. You see him, and you know that he can see you, for you're both out in the free air. All you want to do is ignore this man. Just walk right past him; forget that he had ever existed.

But part of you (perhaps only a small part), at first might want to scoff at him. Just a little. He might not even hear from all the way up on his porch. Maybe you even want to say something to him (something passive-aggressive) because how could he choose to support that absolutely abhorrent politician? Maybe you even feel something growing inside of you. It begins in the pit of your stomach, warming your cheeks, wetting your eyes, gripping your lungs; it makes you want to yell and to cry; it makes you feel five years old, and simultaneously far too old for this world any longer; it makes you hurt; it makes you want to hurt.

Rage.

Hatred.

"I hate you," you want to scream (to hurl your words like spears made to pierce hearts harder than your own).

And now, suppose that this *man*, sitting on his porch (on his throne) so high and mighty in his bigotry, raises his hand at you (a threat? an attack? no it's... a wave). Suppose that this man (this vile old man) waves at you. Greeting you. With a smile.

Maybe he even tosses a friendly, "how are you?"

And how are you? How are you, really?

And what do you do now?

What do you do now?

Well, you can do whatever you want. You've got agency in your own life and this is merely a simulation, an exercise in imagination. If you like to imagine, maybe you can picture a large fire, consuming this man's house (an accident, so they think). But since we're already imagining things, and since (even if only in this instant) you've chosen to be so very brave, when this man waves at you, and he says hello, and he smiles, and he doesn't realize his immense privilege, and he won't acknowledge his complicity in countless injustices, and he refuses to practice basic human empathy—when this man waves at you—I implore you to wave back.

Wave back.

Consider it.

Wave back and remember that his ignorance is not your responsibility.

Wave back and remember that your kindness is a gift, that you are a gift.

Wave back and forget this man.

Wave back.

And then continue walking your dog.

STEP SIX: *Return home.*

Now that your dog is satisfied, and your legs are al dente, you may return home.

And I do hope that you have a home. I hope it's warm and nice.

Someday I'll have to stop over. Maybe someday we could sit together and chat. We could talk about the weather! So temperate lately, am I right? Or we could just sit and not talk. That'd be okay too. Silence is okay, too.

STEP SEVEN: *Prepare for the next walk.*

This was never about one singular walk, of course (but you knew that, didn't you?), because you can never just walk only once; not now that you've got a dog! And a leash! And you've (potentially) greeted your neighbors!

Not now that you've been so very brave and stepped out of your home; not now that you've grown such a fond taste for that which is beyond your place of safety, security, and warmth.

Not now that you've learned how warm the outdoors can feel, when the sun couldn't possibly shine brighter, and for a moment, (even if just for a moment), you can see the beauty of all things, and you remember to breathe, just so you can continue being here, and for now, beautiful.

Not now that you've seen how happy a simple walk around the block can make your friendly little dog.

From now on, you either are walking, or you were walking. From now on, there only is and is between. And do you know what? I think it's just about time for you to walk, again!

Lucky you.

Beautiful you.

First Place—Op-Ed

Nicky Como
Immigration's Effects on Children

In "Contextual Influences on Children's Mental Health and School Performance: The Moderating Effects of Family Immigrant Status," Georgiades et al. discuss the effects immigration has on first-generation/second-generation children's behavior and academic performance, as well as the family processes that may explain these relationships. After gathering research data on 13,470 children aged 4-11 years old in Canada, the authors assert that children of immigrants had fewer emotional/behavioral issues and higher academic performances compared to the nonimmigrant youth in the study (Georgiades et al. 1582). Through other studies, the authors noted that children exposed to more family poverty and neighborhood disadvantages have had negative effects on their mental health. Compared to nonimmigrant youth, immigrant youth were less negatively affected overall (Georgiades et al. 1584). Data for this study was collected for up to four kids per household through a computer-assisted interview with the person most knowledgeable about the child (PMK), usually a parent and/or teacher. A series of ANOVAs (analysis of variance) and chi-square tests were computed to quantify the areas of study. The study sample of immigrant youth was made up of mostly Canadian-born children of immigrant parents (i.e., second-generation children) and about 5% of children were born outside (first-generation) of Canada (Georgiades et al. 1578).

Overall, I agree that the combination of environment and family processes (morals) leads to immigrant youth performing better in school. However, because the PMKs are reporting this study on behalf of their kids, I am not sure how accurate the claim for lack of behavioral issues could be. The term, *behavioral issues* is not well defined in this article. If the term refers to violent outbursts and dangerous behavior, the inferences stand true. However, if the authors include mental health in the term, I will have to disagree with their findings. While they report obvious issues regarding violence and irritability, the PMK cannot measure the mental health of the child with total accuracy. According to this study, I would be considered second-generation. I don't think my mental health was stellar, but I know my parents thought it was normal because I was a well-behaved child. The effects that immigration has on the parents' and childrens' mental health are often overlooked by immigrant parents because of how taboo mental health is considered, which may be a hole in the study. In my experience, I've noticed most foreign parents have never learned about depression or anxiety in an unbiased way. They may not be able to acknowledge that they and/or their children have possibly struggled at some point; this would vary from individual to individual. The authors acknowledged that language barriers and the inability to make causal inferences were study limitations (Georgiades et al. 1588). The aspect that answering mental health questions may have been unreliable should be considered a possible study limitation as well.

Despite the possible flaw with the mental health measurement, this study highlights a prominent aspect of immigration: resilience. The authors state that because familial dysfunctionality may be high, immigrant youth display more resilience due to parenting processes that are supportive of emotional and academic life (Georgiades et al. 1587). More recent immigrant families (defined as less than fifteen years in Canada) have more resilience. Meanwhile, resilience seems to decrease with long-term (immigrant more than fifteen years in Canada) families (Georgiades et al.1574). I've seen this in my life. From my own experience, and through conversations with very recent immigrant families, the desire to achieve is very apparent, and high goals are set.

Research findings in this article suggest that as more years pass from immigration, more behavioral issues may develop. The authors suggest this divergence can occur when the children and the parent are adapting to the new country at different rates (Georgiades et al. 1587). There can be a discrepancy when the children adapt more to the new country while the parents hold on to more traditions from the original country. That discrepancy can create an unspoken dilemma that may lead to more hostile parenting and other problems (Georgiades et al. 1587). I support these claims that the authors made because of my own experience. I was born in America and even though my parents weren't, they had a desire to assimilate. That desire only goes so far, because some key values and traditions they grew up with shall always remain. This leaves it to the second-generation, me in this instance, to accept as much tradition while balancing it with life in America. This also leaves the first-generation, my parents, to try and accept new values while passing down traditions to the next generation. This study shows that years of residency in the new country and the previously mentioned dilemma are positively correlated. As years of residency increase, so does the dilemma of culture clash.

All in all, the authors of "Contextual Influences on Children's Mental Health and School Performance: The Moderating Effects of Family Immigrant Status" correctly identified that recent immigrant families had children with higher school performances and lower behavioral issues. While mental health on the survey collection may have been subjective, the overall findings of this study make sense. This article provides evidence that immigrant children thrive despite economic disadvantages because of the resilience seen in immigrant families. The family processes serve immigrant children well here because parents are very emotionally bonded with their kids, thus guiding them away from behavioral risk problems. I was glad to read an extensive study that focused on the well-being of children affected by immigration. The authors collected this data to present that immigrant children are, overall, resilient despite the obstacles they encounter. It details how there are financial and cultural hurdles, yet immigrant youth are relatively unaffected and persevere. This study provided me with a sense of validation and a new understanding of my life. As a second-generation child, I feel represented by this article.

Work Cited

Georgiades, Katholiki, et al. "Contextual Influences on Children's Mental Health and School Performance: The Moderating Effects of Family Immigrant Status." *Child Development* 78.5 (2007): 1572-1591. Print.

First Place—Poetry

Sanjana Ramanathan
Neon Odyssey

In cities like these, pipelines are convulsing vines
writhing beneath the pulse, the swarm, the stampede of life
on the thin veil of concrete.
Streetlamps flickering staccato
like a heartbeat shudders within each.
When you lie spread eagle on a roof,
on your back with the blur of looming lights
pressing in on your chest,
the familiar ache of fatal telemachy—
even with cotton over your ears,
the screaming traffic below is a siren song.

Cities like these don't sleep but they blink:
quick slivers where reality ceases to exist
for a split-second and a void opens
beneath the sign that sighs DRIVE IN
in stuttering pink.
Magenta cuts through the haze and seeps through your thoughts,
soft like asphalt, spiraling into apologoi.
You'll wish that person you love wasn't too busy
unravelling graffiti in flakes that fall at their feet, afraid
some strange men will call it complete.

In these cities, where hotel rooms are homes
while your home is a place you can't live anymore.
Light refuses your window pane,
gathering out on the fire escape while
swollen shadows of strangers sit at your table.
There's a stillness hanging here:
a notched arrow, a gun's recoil,
shining like the residue of salt water.
Your dreams are a slaughter of the suitors,
blood spilling like dark wine
and dripping through the floorboards,
and your bedroom becomes
Ithaca once more.

Second Place—Poetry

Sophie Geagan
intermission

as spring fluttered in
I fell to hibernation
my eyelids heavy
curled up in the back
flickers of hometown streetlights
fading into view
staying up too late
waking up to midday sun
stabbing at my eyes
staring at posters
curled with age but stubbornly
sticking to the walls
scrolling for hours
careful not to leave a trail
of telltale red hearts
lured out of my bed
only by calls to dinner and
growing restlessness
walking those old streets
greeting every sidewalk crack
like a long-lost friend
turning circles through
neighborhoods I still know well
spinning my own web
forget me for now
maybe someday I'll return
stable, in one piece

Honorable Mention—Poetry

Sophie Geagan
Bloom

I will not bloom.

I will not open my buds and unfurl

my blinding colors like flags

high and proud, no.

I will be an ugly little thing,

my growth stunted from all the times

I tried to cut myself down,

almost passing for a

weed among the flowers

but every day I will

wake with the dawn, look down and

see that my tiny patch of land is still

all mine. I will

dig my roots just a little farther

into the ground. I will

soak up every ray of sunshine and

every drop of rain that comes my way. I will

breathe, and I will

find a way to

survive.

Honorable Mention—Poetry

Muntaha Haq
chocolate princess

i am running on the school track and my feet are pounding against the ground, *left, right, left, right* and i can hear him behind me so i begin to launch like a rocket off the ground but before i can his hand is tight on my wrist and i cannot breathe and he says i am his his his

and i do not like how i can feel his breath warm against my ear or nails dig into my skin

he calls me "chocolate princess" and i feel my stomach lurch at the words

but after practice when he buries his head into my lap and his friends make jokes

i imagine striking you clean in the face, blood gushing out your pretty mouth

sputtering for air as i nail another punch at your hungry, cavernous gut because

if you ever wanted to taste me, consume me, my flavor is not sweet like any chocolate

but instead i rip away from your needy hands and i smile because i am a nice girl

i promise myself that i will not teach my own daughter to be nice

because in this world, a woman can be kind or she can survive

but she cannot have both.

Writers Room

Introduction

Writers Room, now in its eighth year, is a university-community literary arts program engaged in creative place-making and art for social justice. We are a diverse intergenerational collective of students/alumni, faculty/staff, and neighborhood residents whose work demonstrates a desire for collaborative opportunities in our joint communities.

During this year of remote learning, Writers Room created a space, virtually, for writing and conversation. We offered workshops, classes, and student-run open mics. We organized special events with notable authors and produced numerous publications, including *Quaranzine 2020: A New Ritual*. The offerings in this year's *The 33rd* were written by students, alumni, and community writers, and were first published in *Anthology 7*.

Learn more about us at *writersroomdrexel.org*. Beginning in fall of 2021, please join us in our new space in Ross Commons.

—Valerie Fox, Faculty Writing Fellow with Writers Room

Dejah Jade
Hopeless Philly Boy

I wish you knew.

Knew that you could survive

without the feeling to run and hide.

Philly boy.

Stuck with your footprints imprinted in the concrete.

I didn't think when you

marked your name on that concrete

as a kid

you made a deal with the streets.

I hope you know I'm here.

Here to sprinkle my love and protection.

Wishfully thinking that it's enough to shield you.

Shield you from the fate you sadly have already accepted,

that those concrete streets have your name written on.

Destined to have a bullet in that chest

I want to save.

Oh Philly boy,

I miss those days.

Days where I did see

hope in your eyes the younger us that still believed

we could fly.

I see those days have passed you by.

Oh Philly boy.

You're praying for the day that gun hits your flesh

so you can finally rest.

Philly boy just know,

know that I love you.

Alina Macneal
She Made It Look Easy

She made it look easy. Easy to get up at dawn, in the car at six thirty, at work before I'd even gotten up for school.

Before I'd even gotten up for school, she was in the elevator, riding up to the 9th floor in the far back corner.

In the far back corner, where the research labs were, their windows facing light wells and air slots.

Light wells and air slots, where the hospital buildings connected through labyrinths of hallways.

Labyrinths of hallways that I walked during summer vacation, when I was fifteen and sixteen, coming to meet her for lunch.

Sixteen, coming to meet her for lunch, down passageways lined by refrigerators and centrifuges and incubators, and old discarded fume hoods, like somewhere in a dream.

In a dream, years later, I push open a heavy metal door and see her, on a tall stool, in her white lab coat, pipetting from one rack of test tubes to another.

In her white lab coat, pipetting from one rack of test tubes to another, she removes the end of the pipette from her mouth, turns toward me, and smiles. "Did you get lost again?"

Again, I open the door in my dream. Again, she turns toward me and smiles. "No." I say, "I just woke up, like, an hour ago." Again, she laughs.

Kelly Bergh
Once, long, long ago

For a surreal interlude,
Everyone seemed to understand what was about to happen

The man in front of me had a salt-and-pepper beard and a baseball cap,
college-age, cheeks spotted with acne—
divinely empowered to deliver
An eternal, cosmic struggle between good and evil

Rather than defy him, Nearly everybody
Looked at him uncertainly

He flashed an "O.K." hand sign, expressed jubilant surprise
that they were still in charge,
The architects of this apocalypse
Renouncing an entire world view

"It's not a conspiracy when it's documented and recorded."

All language in this poem is taken from "The Storm" by Luke Mogelson, published in *The New Yorker*, January 25, 2021.

Eden Skye Einhorn
Late Night Reflections from a Weary Mind

There's nothing

Except me

At 1 am

2 cans of soda deep into work

For the 3 fittings I have this week

5 garments being made at the same time

Taffeta, cotton, charmeuse, tulle, silk crepe de chine, satin, organza, muslin swatches and pieces scattered around my room

13 hours I've been working nonstop

21 years old and I can't help but wonder about my future

Will it still be like this when I'm 34? Will I be pulling all-nighters before fittings and fashion shows? Will I be pouring my heart and soul into my own designs or will I just be a spare set of hands for someone else?

Will I be happy when I'm 55? Will my dreams have come true? Or will it have been all for nothing? Will I be successful? Will I have reached my goals?

89 years from now I'll be gone. I'll be deep in the dirt, buried in a grave. Will people remember? Will my name still be relevant? Will my clothes still be worn? My name relevant in our culture? Will people know who I was?

I'm dragged out of my thoughts at 144 bpm, courtesy of Nickelback. Right now the future doesn't matter. All that's important is the fabric and the thread in front of me. I can design my future however I please.

Aaliyah Sesay
Easton

When we moved to Easton, my brother Abdul was excited to start the seventh grade at a new school. This was a chance for him to reinvent himself, to become the cool guy and have the cool friends. The brother I lived to impress and defend was scared of the kids at this new school not liking him. And it's hard to imagine that he was so eager to leave his friends. They were always at the house or him at theirs. He explained his need to be liked by the kids at a new school where he would then be seen as the new kid. All that anxious energy amplified when he realized he was new in other senses of the word.

He was among the few black kids in the school, and oftentimes found himself the only one in a classroom. The middle and high school he attended were offensively white. With white kids who would shout, "White Power" on the bus ride home. White kids who scratched confederate flags on lunch room tables. White kids who felt emboldened to say "nigger" to his face, a word they learned on TV, their first introduction to black people before he sat in their class. It was a vast difference from the school he had previously attended, where all his friends were of color except the one white kid who was from the Ukraine. He had been transplanted into a place where the illusion of racial harmony had been dashed.

But he took it all on the chin. When confronted with those racial moments, Abdul engaged in conversations. He spoke to those kids with disturbing calm; like many of us who often find ourselves in spaces where we are outnumbered, he would not let them see his rage, his hurt, his frustration, his disgust. They would not win. So when they make jokes, we laugh to drown out their taunts, to obfuscate frustrated tears with those of laughter. Laughter masks a crumbling much easier than a smile. When they said "nigga" or "nigger," Abdul stayed in the moment, asking why they felt it was okay to use it. But above all the ways in which he dealt with his peers, he silently and unwittingly promised himself he would never give them a reason to use it on him.

Abdul recounted an interaction with a white kid on the bus: the kid asked him, "How did your parents afford to buy the house you live in? Selling drugs?" An odd question, Abdul responded, "No. Not all black people mess with crack."

He remembers many moments like this, explaining and deconstructing their misconceptions of black people. That responsibility they threw on him to be the voice, translator, commentator on all things black he says he gratefully took because he knew someone had to do it. Which is understandable, but he's not friends with these kids today. He wasn't really friends with them at the time either. He had found the group of black kids that moved into the development and they became his circle. And throughout all these years, Abdul managed to maintain contact with his buddies back in Ewing. Like ebbs and flows, these boys, now men, have remained friends.

Our school district, Wilson Area, is fairly small. There are three regional elementary schools that students attend based on where they live: Williams Township, Wilson, and Avona. Once they start middle school, all those students are shoved into the middle and high school. Because it is such a densely populated location, students living in the Wilson area are split into Wilson and Avona. This area of town is typically denoted as the more urban. When I started middle school, I was often asked where in Wilson I lived and if I went to Wilson or Avona, because other students hadn't seen me before and I was black. Blacks, apparently, are only native to urban areas. Just a microcosm of racial profiling I would experience at a young age. Williams Township, on the other hand, was much more rural. Students from those areas were either well-off with big houses and lots of land or of lower-income but still had lots of land. The students and families here tended to be white, except for us and a handful of other black and Asian families. Our family lived in one of the two developments in Williams Township, which mirrored the suburbs with a more rural spin on it.

This made riding the bus hell. Sometimes students would forget that black kids sat on the same bus as them, in the seat in front of them. I remember kids making jokes about where I should sit on the bus, which made me wonder too. The front because so many had fought for my right to do that or the back because that was the new front, where all the cool kids sat? Our access to "coolness" and popularity was denied because we were black. Automatically relegated to the front or back or wherever they say because who wants to be friends with the black kid. Sometimes, kids would make it a game to stick as many pencils in my hair as they could and see how long it took me to notice. Extra points if it managed to stay throughout all the bumpy roads.

I've fought against anger because I know how it makes me look: Angry Black Girl, burnt and bitter. How I wish I could be sweet and light and inoffensive to the senses, but I'm not. I've lived with a lot of pent up rage. Rage toward the white kids at school. Who made me change the way I talk to hide, to survive. Who stuck pencils in my hair. Who said my hair reminded them of a dog named "Frou Frou" but when it was straightened I looked like "them," like a person. Who told me I was a different kind of black. It took me over ten years for me to understand how my teachers were apathetic toward me, no matter how much I tried to make myself stand out. I would take refuge in my room because I wasn't sure if the other kids liked me, not sure why I couldn't just fit in. So many prayers spent on making a friend, just one to make me feel less lonely. Daily prayers, nightly prayers. Prayers so silent they don't even reach the mind, birthed in our hearts and dead in our tears.

/ Faculty Writing

Introduction

Faculty writing reflects current, published work by professors in the College of Arts and Sciences. These texts have previously appeared in academic journals, books, conferences, magazines, newspapers, and websites. They are often thought-provoking, poignant, and funny, and they serve as a powerful demonstration of the many forms that writing can take. *The 33rd* is enriched by the interests and passions of these writers.

—*The Editors*

Jan Armon
Rob—A Flash Memoir

It was late '98, not yet time to party like it's 1999. I was having lunch with my wife's sister and her three children. The eldest, Rob, was in his second year at Indiana University. In the midst of our sandwiches, Paula breaks out in a tirade against Rob for not using protection during sexual activity. It's amazing what a mother learns. Her 6 foot 5 inch son cringed, for she'd nailed him. But I could see that yelling at him was not going to work. By the time he returned to I.U., my nephew would continue taking risks.

When lunch ended I said to Rob, let's take a walk. He said, okay uncle Jan, and we walked quietly for a few minutes. Then I said, during my twenties I didn't use protection, Rob; I was that stupid. The 1970s were a time when women were pressured to use the pill and a few ridiculous devices—none of which protected them from disease, I added.

One day, Rob, I ran into a woman I'd dated a few times a few years previously. She said she had tickets for a play and invited me to go with her that evening. It was a fine performance of *The Rainmaker*. You should see it sometime. Afterwards we went back to her apartment. Remember what I told you, Rob. Guys assumed that women took care of birth control. But I paused and asked her, you're using birth control, aren't you?

Oh, don't worry, she said. I can't get pregnant. The moon is in Taurus.

And that, Rob, is why the Zodiac is bullshit and you should always, always wear a condom. Okay? Okay, uncle Jan, said Rob.

Valerie Fox
Interpretation, for Bliss

 Aquarian, old friend, a dream of water points to a harmless failure in baking, to three magic chords, to getting a cat (Donna), to Donna turning into a fish and then, into a filigreed vessel, covered in gold lamé, decorated with sleep, so get to it. Stay safe.

Valerie Fox
Our Komodo (A Kind of Love)

Mrs. Komodo, at Home

You said you'd be right back. I await. Up a tree. All our grinning kids are gone. I don't let the watchers get close. Four of those dirty beasts perch with their binoculars and tuna-fish sandwiches. Yum. I'm afraid. I hear scratching and tapping. Like dental or scissors. They mention you are at Disney World and laugh. I'm queasy. I miss your serrated bites. I don't feel like hunting anymore, I'm hurting. I've got my soaps and trailing yarn. Maybe that's enough. I fell hard for your handsome gait. I took care of the kids. You said a minute.

Abstract

Our lizards are shy, an island animal. Here's a nest decoy. Our young have wrinkles all around their baby eyes. They're used to us and their drastic teeth are changing year by year.

This juvenile one is April Jo. Still residing, at seven years, she has her own tree-view. Her waddle is fetching, her grin. As she grows up, we measure April Jo's envenomed, gripping bite.

Many tests in hill-stations use goats. The meat attracts *Varanus komodoensis*. Same thing with lookalike automatic menus. Look, that's where we put the goats. We aren't doing that as much anymore since, honestly, our friends come to expect this meat offering and lose some of their hiding and hunting ways. You want to adapt a little or at least to try.

Check out her rotational chewing point, that vector. She has her mama's eyes. Is anyone else here feeling lonely or sleepy?

The effort to survive airplanes is intense. That's the second one today. Bacteria survive and colonize. Here we say "disease" without meaning positive or negative. Mortal, not moral. Bacteria stay in the mouth and on escaped prey. In the next activity we will join forces and form a grid. Later we'll plug in our numbers.

One favorite study is like this. You approach an individual to see how long it takes the giant to react. "To react" means to turn and look, gaze. Keep your handwriting steady. You want your notes to be legible. If there's enough time we'll come back. You can guess what we mean by enough time.

We get enchanted by the direction of what we are gathering here, and we are going to go full on and four-footed. We are not a zoo. Let's break for lunch. *Be quiet for now, stay frozen.*

Mr. Komodo, Extant for Now

I didn't choose this side of the planet, I was drugged, awoke in this bacteria-free condo. Inhaled the refrigerator contents lickety-split and scratched the sofa-back raw. Can't get these claws to work the buttons on things. Worst part is seeing clever you on-screen. And the kids, alert on their puffy, sun-filled bellies. A few limbs and branches were dangling from your dear mouth. As part of this new life there are too many kinds of milk substitutes and banknotes, so it gets super confusing. I think away my days. I whine at you on the elephantine TV: *I am glad you'll never see me this way*. I yearn to hear the voice of someone who still has a heart.

Jordan Hyatt
Send First Vaccines to Pennsylvania's Prisons

Pennsylvania's prisons and jails have been ravaged by COVID-19. Incarcerated people, and the staff who supervise them, were among the first to suffer in the pandemic. They should also be among the first to be vaccinated, not only for their benefit but to protect the broader community.

For example, over half of the people incarcerated at State Correctional Institute Laurel Highlands have recently tested positive for COVID-19. This is especially frightening because this facility functions as a correctional nursing home for the sickest and oldest incarcerated people. Correctional staff has also been hit hard, creating an environment that is universally stressful and potentially dangerous. Other prisons have been similarly impacted, with an increasing amount of staff and incarcerated people testing positive.

From a public health perspective, prisons are unique. Behind their walls, it can be impossible to socially distance; almost everyone has a cellmate, eating is designed up to be communal, and bathrooms are shared by dozens. Security restrictions prevent using the type of alcohol-based disinfectants that have become the norm in the community. Older facilities are poorly ventilated. The high population density creates an ideal environment for the spread of disease.

As a population, incarcerated people are particularly susceptible to coronavirus. In addition to the challenges created by their environments, many people who are incarcerated have pre-existing health conditions that make them vulnerable to serious infection and long-term complications. As a result, incarcerated people are four times more likely to die of COVID-19.

Last week, the National Academies of Sciences, Engineering, and Medicine released a framework for vaccine distribution. Adopting a primarily ethical perspective, it determined that incarcerated people should receive the vaccine early because they live in "congregate or overcrowded settings including … prisons, or jails." This would place them in the second wave, alongside nursing home residents, but after front-line health workers.

This means that people in prison might get the vaccine before you and I do. Though perhaps counterintuitive to some, this is both ethical and in everyone's best interest.

While it is true that people in prison may have broken the law, dying of COVID-19 is not a part of their sentence. While they have lost their liberty, and that is their true punishment, we have a moral and constitutional obligation to keep them safe while they serve that punishment.

Practically, vaccinating the entire incarcerated population is necessary to stop community spread. Absent universal vaccination, prisons will continue to be a source of infection. Staff, chaplains, and visitors enter prisons every day. When they return to their neighborhoods, so will the coronavirus. This is true for prisons in both rural and urban areas; the impact is nearly universal.

Correctional staff also deserve to work in an environment that is as safe as possible. Until the vast majority of incarcerated people are vaccinated, staff will remain at risk. The high rates of infection among correctional employees underscores the risk they bear and our obligation to protect them.

Simply put, society cannot continue to act as if incarcerated people and the general public suffer from two separate pandemics. As wards of the state, the costs of treating incarcerated people, one should remember, are ultimately borne by taxpayers and will require the diversion of significant resources from our already overburdened community hospitals.

The time for action is now. Other states have started to consider how, when, and even if, incarcerated people should be given access to a vaccine when it becomes available. Unsurprisingly, reactions are polarized. In Connecticut, for example, incarcerated people will be included in the second wave of distribution, along with nursing home residents and others living in "congregate settings." In Colorado, on the other hand, the Governor has made clear that incarcerated people should be among the last to be vaccinated.

To protect all Pennsylvanians, we simply must vaccinate the entire incarcerated population as soon as is possible.

This action will help stop the spread of COVID-19 in prisons and from prisons back into the rest of society. Failing to do so would endanger marginalized communities that are both overrepresented in the penal system and have been hardest hit by the COVID crisis—and prevent us all from moving safely forward.

Henry Israeli
To Have Lived Long Enough To Be Allowed To Return

I couldn't sleep so I got up and walked out onto the street

where I saw gathered in small circles on every lawn

wild animals—rabbits, skunks, deer, vole,

cats, and owls of every shape and size,

even a few red foxes with little black gloves—all speaking

an English of a curious vernacular, a kind of under-the-din pub talk

complete with four-pint-slur and cigarette snarl,

but as I approached they dispersed, pretending

to be fearful or unfriendly, their eyes darting around

to avoid my gaze, muttering inaudibly,

so I lay down in the middle of the road, hoping to blend

into the asphalt and listen to the wisdom of my mammalian cousins

who gathered around me, sniffing my ears,

poking me with snouts and beaks, and then a cloud of bats

descended from the sky, gathering me up by my pajamas,

lifting me into the air and carrying me off to a damp cave

where a small fire illuminated a kind of diorama:

my father sitting on an oversized chair watching

Cronkite on TV, my mother in the kitchen just out of sight,

frozen in the midst of shaping ground carp

into little balls with her bare hands, the soaring colors of 1975

blossoming on the wallpaper around us.

When the bats gently dropped me onto the shag carpet

I closed my eyes and breathed in my childhood as deeply as I could,

my first home, the egg that long ago hatched me,

kingdom of my body, my pain, my nocturnal delirium.

Kirsten Kaschock
The Urgency of Being

Louise Bourgeois, the artist, is no longer. She died in 2010 at the age of 98.

Louise Bourgeois is no longer, except.

I met Bourgeois's work in 1999 when I was 27, just becoming an adult through motherhood (she and I both gave birth to three sons). Her art made me feel like a child on the cusp of unchildhood. I can't tell you why exactly. Her line drawings are simple, witty, sometimes engaging in the visual equivalent of wordplay: a skyscraper with legs, a woman's face echoed by a cat's. They tend to hint at the types of darkness you can find in most houses: spiders and dark windows, mothers and scissors and hair. Maybe you knew a child like me, one who didn't know why they hurt so much. I felt like Bourgeois knew, or was, a child like me—the way I was at 11.

When I first saw her work it was in a book filled with her drawings, though she was best known as a sculptor. I read the things she said about those drawings, words about art that was not her "main" art. Some of her words have burrowed into me.

These are maggots. It looks like a very negative subject. In fact, it is not a negative subject at all. In fact, if I were religious, I would say that it is the theme of the resurrection.

I met up with Bourgeois's work again at an exhibition at MoMA, "Louise Bourgeois: An Unfolding Portrait," in late 2017 and felt 27 again—the age I turned, because of motherhood, away from dance and into words.

Looking at her repetitive drawings (figures and structures both organic and architectural), at a single example of her immense welded spiders (I've met two before), and at a few of her "cells" (life-sized emotional microcosms, one-person rooms, psychological set-pieces), I felt like a child again. Enraged, entranced, shot-through, riddled with the needles of her lifelong practice (she began drawing to help her parents in their tapestry-repair business). That day, I felt like 27-year-old me re-feeling my own particular brand of 11-year-old pain. In actuality I was four times that age.

In a single body, there hide any number of childhoods. Maturity, I think, is a myth. And time—an illusion made impossible to treat as illusion by aging. The containment of our bodies in space is part of what creates the fantasy of space. Our bodies' housing of other bodies (fetuses and tumors alike) fosters still other kinds of delusion: immortality, cessation. Bourgeois knew this. She refused to let her own work travel in only one direction. She redrew the same line drawings dozens of times over decades. A famous installation of her architectural sculptures at the Tate Modern was titled *I do, I undo, I redo.* Her spirals, whether enormous staircase or tiny shell, point out over-and-over again that time and growth do not move as we perceive them to.

Maggots know this also.

Mostly Bourgeois plumbs and replumbs distinctly domestic and bodily horrors. At least, that is how her work speaks to me—in dark fables that return me to a time when every word and object and gesture held magic, which is the illimitable potential for beauty and terror both. After childhood, every demon or angel that an artist seeks to manifest must be wrested from the aether, and because we are the creators, we know they are not real. And because we are the creators, what we make is more real to us than anything else could ever be.

My friend Sarah Jane is dying, has been living the end of her life for over two years now, but cancer is all through her and is not receding. Nothing stops her from savoring life. Recently, as she drank the heavy cream she imbibes to keep any kind of weight on her body, she said to me, "People wonder how I am still alive: I love living." Then she turned her face to the sky, closed her eyes, and smiled like a cat. Suddenly, the sun was on my skin. I felt it. When I am in her presence, cancer is contagious. And it bestows not its pain but its only blessing: an urgency of being.

I arrived at the University of Iowa in the fall of 1996 with a shaved head. Ours was love at first sight: the flame-haired ballerina and me—the modern dance choreographer with the gymnast build—we were the only grad students entering the MFA program that August. We admired each other across the classroom. It didn't take long before she adopted me, but then Sarah Jane adopted all the strays.

Strong, lithe, sparking: she seemed a creature who thought with her body. I soon learned she had a master's degree in math. She grew up in Buffalo, NY, but had relocated to Iowa from New Orleans. There was a sadness to her eyes that seemed a necessary corollary to her room-lighting smile. That first month, she asked me if I wanted to do acid on a Saturday when we didn't have rehearsal (our schedule was grueling). I said yes.

After that, I was a constant staple at her place—the House Dubuque—an ex-dentist's office now three-bedroom-apartment on the street that led to the university. When the growing bunch of us, all misfits, hung out late nights on the porch, we could count on undergraduates passing by in affable stumble. My dorm was a mile-and-a-half up the river, the walk cold and lonely, so I slept on the couch of House D often, then moved on to the carpeted bedroom floor of my future husband, Danny. He was one of Sarah Jane's housemates, another adoptee, a cell geneticist.

Two years ago, Sarah arrived at our house in Philly on the way to upstate New York to see her parents. We have visited each other so sporadically in the decades since Iowa, you might think it'd be awkward. With SJ—nothing is. She showed me the chest port recently installed for her chemotherapy. At her insistence, she and I went dancing to Balkan music by the river while Danny watched the kids.

Sarah is dying. This past July she turned 51. I doubted she would see this birthday—I was wrong. For two decades she seemed to age neither in physique nor peterpannish demeanor, remaining the age she was when I fell in love with her. I think now, like the title character of her favorite childhood book, *The Little Prince*, that she was loaned to us.

• • •

In October of 2017, I climbed onto an early morning bargain bus from Philadelphia to New York.

The bus ride was a spontaneous decision. I didn't teach that day and I'd found out about the Bourgeois exhibition at MoMA from a friend on social media. I desperately wanted to go. My sister Taryn was in New York. We planned a lunch date.

I had too much coffee that morning. As a result, I had to use the bus toilet. A sudden stop made us lurch, and the underwear I'd pulled down below my knees got splashed. Soaked. For a few moments I had no idea what to do. Then I yanked them off, threw them away and cleaned my legs with a startling amount of hand sanitizer. I walked around the city all day in a knee-length skirt sans drawers.

I tell you this because they are important—bodily facts.

My body exists in the midst of chaos, and the way it encounters the world affects my functioning within it. Undoubtedly. But nothing was going to stop me from seeing my favorite artist's work. Not uncomfortable travel, not the difficulty of reorganizing my children's schedules (their father Danny spends half the week in an apartment in DC), not assault by the Bolt Bus's blue water. Not shame.

Despite the traffic, the bus arrived early, so I decided to walk the thirty blocks uptown. My crotch was cold. My sister and I met up in the lobby and entered the museum. She didn't know Bourgeois's work but she knew I did. It was crowded, and as we moved through the rooms, we read, we looked, we spoke, and we took pictures of each other beside the pieces. Taryn said she felt like she was walking around inside my brain. I felt like that too. So familiar yet un-. I have never documented a trip through art so thoroughly. I knew I wanted to be able to go back, to revisit the drawings: simple lines depicting boxes and buildings, faces and figures, organic shapes and scissors, threaded knots and bodies bent in half. I am not a fine artist, and I've never wanted to buy a catalogue of one's work, but I wanted documentation of this. All of it. An archive. Are such desires a function of my increasing age? A developing sense of mortality? Is this why all museums feel old—not because of what is in them, but because of the curators' desires to contain and catalogue, to prove by sheer quantity that a life matters? That art does?

Luckily, I found an interactive listing of Bourgeois's drawings and prints online that contains more art, even some of her words. So after I returned from the show, I dug further into Bourgeois's themes and variations: what I like to think of as her near-century-long barre work.

• • •

In ballet, a barre is a stationary handrail, often attached to a wall, where dancers go to perform the repetitive daily exercises that keep them strong and flexible, aiding them in perfecting a bodily technique that is anything but natural.

I grew up at the barre. So did my sister Taryn. So did Sarah Jane.

During college, it became difficult for me to square my developing feminism with my love of ballet. I should never have liked ballet—its strict gender roles, its hierarchical ranks, its imposition of impossible and unhealthy body ideals upon (mostly) young women. And in fact, I did hate it, for a time. And then I met Sarah Jane.

The feminists took me as a role model, as a mother. It bothers me. I am not interested in being a mother. I am still a girl trying to understand myself. -LB

With her, from her, in class beside her for two years, I learned that there was a way to get beneath the horror of a thing and to its beauty (always intertwined). And that the path was an obsessive dedication to understanding form: both the human form and its desire to direct itself through chosen (not compulsory) behavior. To become something else, to do something else other than what is expected, to grow in a different way than the given.

What could be more feminist than that?

• • •

Louise Bourgeois, like Sarah Jane, first went to school as a mathematician before turning her attention to her art. I can feel a mathematician's sensibility in her work. The rationality is visceral. It is procedural. It is balletic. One tries the most nuanced permutations, algorithms painstakingly designed to unlock the way forward. One goes away and one returns, again and again, to the scene of the crime. Which is always, already, and again childhood. First position, second. Fifth. Every day of a dancer's life is in some ways the day she began her training—the same exercises: plié, tendu, rond de jambe.

Ballet can be a home that resembles a prison, and the only way to escape its claustrophobic form is to inhabit it so fully that you pupate, and so are transformed.

This is the dream, I think.

I think Bourgeois dreamt it too. I have heard her reproductions of her childhood residence and its formative scenes of infidelity and illness called obsessive. I think of it simply as the work. In the work, you can find beauty and horror, meaning and purpose. But the work does not give any answer other than this one: you must keep at it.

• • •

So it means that however hard things are, there is still hope if you believe in maggots. Something has decomposed, and it is from that decomposition that hope comes again. –LB

Sarah Jane is dying. Her body would not be directed by her to heal—and yet. She is not dying in the way anyone expected. Over the past year, I have traveled down to see her in New Orleans half a dozen times. Each time there is less of her, and still there is all of her.

I stayed with her for ten days this summer, allowing her sister Julia to take a week in Buffalo with her son and husband before returning to care for her sister. Sarah Jane and Julia are teaching me about what a sister is and sometimes has to be. The horror is not something they shirk from; their gallows humor walks hand-in-hand with the most tender expressions I have ever seen exchanged between non-lovers. I am grateful for these lessons. While I was there, SJ taught ballet in the front room of her house, as she has been doing for the past few years, to four adult students and me, and by Skype to our old housemate from Iowa, Amy. The way she moves her arms and back is still a miracle, though now you can watch each tendon ripple across her deltoids when she demonstrates. SJ is near skeletal and wears a colostomy bag because tumors have gathered in her lungs and abdomen. At last imaging, the largest of the thirty or so was the size of a grapefruit. When she made poop jokes, all the women in the room laughed. Throughout the week, SJ and I talked bedsores and front-farts and hemorrhoids and droopy, chafed vulvas.

I tell you this because they are inescapable and brutal and hilarious and she lists hers without shame—bodily facts.

We also binged Netflix and ate paleo-cookies. Sometimes there were tears. Sometimes rage. Love, always.

• • •

Our body is a home we traverse and decorate and renovate until we can't. One of Bourgeois's most iconic images is called "Femme Maison." In it, the bottom half of a woman protrudes from what appears a large dollhouse. Two arms extend from the walls. The arms are doll-sized and one is waving.

When my sister saw that particular drawing at MoMA, she said: "I get it."

I think she meant me—that she gets me. And she does. But what is there to get? That I feel trapped in my domesticity? In my childhood? That I think my hips are too big for the front door? Or that I will never not-view everything in my world as a metaphor for everything else?

After our visit to Bourgeois, Taryn and I went to sit and have lunch and talk about lives that seem to keep spiraling beyond our control. We are both teachers, and mothers. We both hate the direction our country seems committed to. We both take solace in the students we see daily—dancers and writers, scientists and mathematicians—and we are committed to them and to our own art.

She asked me then—because she asks me every time we speak, because she is my sister, because she gets me—how Sarah Jane was doing. I gave her the same answer on that October day that I give today: "She is dying. So are you. So am I."

Every day that Taryn goes to the barre, each day I sit down with pen and paper, each day SJ lifts her face to the sun—is a day to construct, deconstruct, reconstruct.

We do, we undo, we redo.

Miriam N. Kotzin
Cairn

    Unless she deviates from the prescribed route, Sarah's GPS will have her drive past her parents, and, although she hasn't visited since her mother's birthday and, months before that, an anniversary, she doesn't want to stop today, and, besides, soon it will be dark, and not having planned for this, she isn't properly dressed (denim shorts, sleeveless blouse, sandals), nor does she have anything to leave, not one stone, and how can she go without a stone to leave behind for them and as proof for anyone who might come by later that someone (else) cared enough to visit, so she needs a stone to leave even though over the decades she's left hundreds that might've made a proper cairn as a grave marker and also, as she knew (and found amusing), a trail marker for a trail that leads only below ground, and, because, after the ceremonies of her mother's funeral, she'd waited while the gravediggers finished their work, she's taken a sneak peek into her own spot in the pit that she sees whenever she kneels to trim back the aggressive crabgrass growing over the granite markers, and now that she's an old woman herself, her parents are in all her nightmares, standing by, smiling and silent, but when she's awake their indistinct voices rise and fall like music on a radio in the next room, so she signals and turns into the cemetery drive, and the GPS says, "Recalculating, recalculating" in her mother's most beautiful clear voice.

Miriam N. Kotzin
Covid-19 2020

The young father presses his hands flat against the window. Although the mask covers half his face, the baby knows him. New game. Laughing, she reaches for the father's hands, cool glass between them.

She lifts her arms, "Up." Old game.

The father's learned the new rules: he turns away.

Miriam N. Kotzin

I Tell My Therapist That My Mother's Lessons Didn't Hold Water

Leafy sunlight on his garden wall. Ripples in river shallows. Shadows on clay riverbed.

"My mother made pots with river clay. She taught me to weave and to carry water in baskets."

Pine Barrens cedar water runs clear and dark. "But all that happened when I was only a girl."

Miriam N. Kotzin
That Takes the Cake

During the war and post-war sugar rationing, my mother struggled to satisfy Dad's sweet tooth. On his 40th birthday, she flourishes Fanny Farmer's Boston Cooking School Cookbook, his mother's engagement gift, to announce that she's making a "real birthday cake. Not one drop of corn syrup!"

She'd kept her scheme secret. She could've told me—I wouldn't have ruined her surprise.

Dad chuckles, asking if Mom used a gun to hold up the Piggly Wiggly, or if she was only turning into a grifter.

Mom blushes and tells us how she was in the baking aisle checking her shopping list when she realized she'd forgotten the ration book, and she started to bawl. She told a solicitous woman she had everything for Dad's birthday cake at home—except sufficient sugar. That woman got busy until just about everybody gave Mom sugar, tablespoon by tablespoon.

Mom has just enough sugar and time to bake Dad's cake before dinner. Busy with flour, measuring cups, and bowls, she asks me to take the butter, milk, and eggs out of the fridge.

Wishing she'd told me her plan, apprehensive, I put the butter and milk on the table.

"Eggs," she prompts. "I need eggs for the cake."

I reach into the fridge and pull out all our eggs, now on a large plate covered by a sheet of waxed paper, my father's favorite savory snack: deviled eggs.

After one grim moment, Mom laughs. She checks Farmer's index—Voilà! a recipe for eggless chocolate cake.

Lynn Levin
Dr. Rieux, Meet Dr. Fauci: Seeing Albert Camus's *The Plague* with 2020 Vision

In the summer of 2020, seventeen Drexel University students, many of them international students, Zoomed into my Great Works class to explore Albert Camus' *The Plague*. The students found themselves amazed at how eerily this World War Two allegory paralleled our own struggle with Covid-19. Many characters in the novel endure quarantine, exile, and the pain of separation from loved ones, and so did a number of my students. Camus describes many of his characters' actions as expressing the best of humanity; similarly, my students gained a sense of optimism as they observed empathy and solicitude of doctors and nurses, the tireless service of sanitation workers, and everyday people sharing kindnesses. These and other parallels made reading this masterpiece a real-life experience for us. The line between the novel and now became porous. Of course, we were not caught in an actual war, but we were fighting on four fronts: the coronavirus, the state of the economy, the cultural upheaval of the Black Lives Matter movement, and the looming presidential election. Guiding students through this novel at this time—and, just as often, standing back to listen in amazement to their insights and debates—was easily the most exciting experience of my twenty years of teaching.

Both a philosophical inquiry and a novel of action, *The Plague* is set in the then-French Algerian town of Oran, which is in the grip of an epidemic of the bubonic plague. The gruesome and agonizing disease allegorizes the German occupation of France; the fight against it, undertaken by medical doctors and citizen volunteers, represents the French resistance. The quarantine that health authorities institute to contain the epidemic echoes border closures during the occupation, a type of imprisonment that forces loved ones to live apart in loneliness and longing, or, as Camus often puts it, to linger in a state of exile.

I had taught the novel several times before, but grappling with the book in past years, intellectually exciting as it was, was a historical and academic experience. Whenever we talked about epidemics of the past, such as the actual black death, polio, malaria, zika, the influenza of 1918, or even HIV/AIDS, our discussions felt safe, remote, even antiseptic. Now, however, we were in the midst of our own plague, and our perceptions were extraordinarily sharpened. We came to read the book as a chronicle of our own experience. So immersed were the students in the now of the book, that I periodically had to call the class's attention to Camus's subtle and not-so-subtle references to Nazism, the Holocaust, the occupation, and the resistance. As electrical engineering major Christina Strobel wrote, "I found it absolutely fascinating that everything Camus described was what we went through in our own pandemic. He would describe things, and I would think 'I've been there,' or 'I've felt that.' I kept having to remind myself that Camus hadn't actually witnessed what the world is going through today."

Because many of my students lived abroad or had family in other countries, they related keenly to pain of separation that many of Camus's characters feel as they find themselves trapped in quarantined Oran. A biomedical engineering student, Kebeh Maryann Oden said, "It is hard being away from my family. My mum is in Nigeria, and we try to talk every day, but it is hard. Summer was the time for all my family to come together and enjoy time with each other." Muhammad Ubaid Ullah, an economics and finance major, was in a similar situation. "I think I am living in exile. Sure, today's lockdown is not comparable to the one in Oran, but I'm still locked away from Pakistan, my home. I can video call my family to talk, but I cannot be with them in a time they need me emotionally." American students writing from the States did not feel exiled, but they certainly felt lonely. The people in Oran mostly had to rely on ten-word telegrams to reach others out of town. All the students marveled at how much easier it was for us with Internet and cell phones, even though our technological marvels could not fully resolve separation anxiety and loneliness. As data science major Palash Pandey, now back home in India, observed, "All the tech in the world can't help you when you're stranded in an airport worrying if immigration will let you through."

The book follows the tireless efforts of the book's protagonist, Dr. Bernard Rieux as he attempts to tend to the victims of the plague. Who was our Dr. Rieux? Hands down, it was Dr. Anthony Fauci, everyone in the class agreed. His was the voice of sanity and reason, always serving, always there to protect the public's health. Old Dr. Castel who tries and tries to develop anti-plague serum mirrors our medical researchers who are racing to develop treatments and vaccines for Covid-19.

And who comprised our "sanitary squads," the citizen volunteers organized by Dr. Rieux's friend Tarrou to help combat the plague by transporting victims and improving health conditions, risking infection as they worked? (In the book, these teams represent the French resistance.) Everyone immediately said they were the health care workers, the guys who hauled away our trash, the food processing workers, indeed, all the essential workers who often were putting their lives on the line to care for us and feed us. I named as our class's own "Tarrou" student Amber Bolli, a biology major and aspiring veterinarian who is serving as a volunteer contact tracer in the state of Pennsylvania. Maybe I overdid it. Despite the distance of Zoom, I think I saw Amber shrink from my praise. Palak Bhargava, an engineering and math major from New Delhi, said, "Custodians were the ultimate yet the most underrated sanitary squad workers. The people who wipe our floors and hallways, pick up our garbage, clean our sewers and do much more—all without a sliver of praise." And while Camus demurs from overpraising as heroes people who are simply doing what basic common decency demands, the students nevertheless honored as heroes all the essential workers who served us diligently in our time of plague.

In the novel, a combination of coming cold weather, a possible weakening of the disease, and Dr. Castel's newest serum puts an end to the epidemic. Speaking through Dr. Rieux, who has endured the deaths of many including those dearest to him, Camus concludes with a call to vigilance and a declaration of hope for humankind, stating "quite simply what we learn in time of pestilence: that there are more things to admire in men than to despise." Most students drew from the book a sense of optimism and pointed out how many people showed their good sides in this time of coronavirus and civil unrest. Once again, all the students spoke of their admiration for the doctors and nurses, delivery drivers, sanitation workers, and other essential personnel who kept us functioning during these fraught months. Audrey Coffey, a psychology major living in the suburbs of Philadelphia, praised those protesting in support of Black Lives Matter and those checking in on loved ones. Tommy Nguyen, a computer science major from the Chicago area, expressed cautious optimism as he spoke about "non-profits and governmental organizations coming together to create policies to help people in need." Among such uplifting measures, he listed "pauses on evictions, stimulus checks… and people cleaning up broken glass after the George Floyd riots." Ultimately, he said, *The Plague* made him more optimistic about overcoming the Covid-19 pandemic. Other class members praised people who sewed masks and made charitable contributions. Several students pointed out that the stay-at-home guidelines enabled them to get to know themselves and their partners better. A few also noted that the lockdown triggered some divorces.

Tarik Kose, an information systems major residing in Philadelphia wrote, "Despite all the negativity around the virus and people who aren't doing their part, but are instigating further negativity, there are many slivers of positivity that give me hope." He also drew the distinction between "plagues of the flesh" over which we have little control and "plagues that darken our hearts"—these, he said, are the ones we have some power to avoid. Christina Strobel, the electrical engineering major, for whom the book had an uncanny way of expressing many of her feelings, wrote, "We don't need to be saints or doctors, just people who know what we are capable of," people who are aware "that we only have a limited time to relieve as much suffering as possible."

When the town of Oran announces the official end of the plague, citizens swarm the streets in celebration, a scene reminiscent of rejoicing at the liberation of Paris. This August, there was a massive pool party in Wuhan, China where revelers celebrated the city's bounce back from the health crisis. Quite a few class members debated the rights and wrongs of the Wuhan pool party. Would there, I asked, be dancing in the streets when we get a Covid-19 vaccine? I do not recall any of the students' thinking that huge public celebrations would erupt in America, though one person said that he expected some wild times at private parties and in bars. Mostly the students expected a muted response, stating what many health authorities have told us, that the coronavirus would continue to live among us. For as Camus says, referring doubly to reigns of terror and onslaughts of disease, "the plague bacillus never dies or disappears for good." Aarnav Chauhan, a finance and business analytics major from Mumbai, observed that we can never truly consider ourselves free of pandemics. "In 2020," he wrote, "we are still completely unprepared for an event that has occurred at least every century for several centuries."

Still, the students hung on to a prevailing belief in human goodness. Just as Camus maintains that there are "more things to admire in men than to despise," Amber Bolli, the biology major and volunteer contact tracer, summed it up best: "Our biggest takeaway from this novel and in our current times, is just how well humanity can come together in times of need."

It's always the right time to read or teach Albert Camus's *The Plague*. This year, however, the masterpiece astounds and enlightens more than ever.

George A. MacMillan
Fighting Solo: Covid-19 and the Single Parent

The COVID-19 crisis has brought about an era of self-imposed isolation many of us have never known. We have become refugees in our own homes, estranged from our modern lifestyles and all its conveniences. While technology has held the fabric of our society close in some social and economic circles, it has failed to prevent many from feeling isolated. Certain populations are at a higher risk of economic damage and loss of personal safeties brought about by this isolation. One such population, often unmentioned in media coverage of the pandemic, is that of single-parent households.

Earlier this year, through a series of dire circumstances, my daughters and I joined the statistics of single-parent households in the United States. According to the U.S. Census Bureau, as of 2016, there were eleven million single-parent households in the U.S.[1] The reasons behind this are many, ranging from the death of a partner/spouse to divorce, abandonment and, most tragically, domestic violence. The rise of the single-parent household in the U.S. is a specter which continues to haunt American family life and is inapposite to the family values charade bandied about by politicians and religious leaders.

What the COVID-19 crisis has shown is how quickly our accustomed quality of life can decline when modern conveniences, often taken for granted, are stripped away. For any family, dealing with the pandemic can be both emotionally and financially draining. For the working single parent, it beckons a heightened level of crisis in that childcare may be lost, the security provided by school meals is removed, and families on the verge of financial collapse are catapulted over its edge. Furthermore, many single-parent households are also dealing with issues of personal safety now magnified by the crisis. On top of that, there are the routines of daily living that are no longer routine. They have become an almost insurmountable burden.

For most, the social distancing restrictions in place are no more than a nuisance: long lines at grocery stores, takeout dining in lieu of restaurant seating, and closed social venues. Many still enjoy the conveniences of modern living. In fact, for some, the pandemic has become an imposed vacation of sorts. For many Americans, their incomes have not been affected—yet. For them, finances remain stable, food is on the table, and "necessary" trips to stores (as loosely as this term has come to be understood) carry on. All the while, the costs of employment for many have been negated, from commuting to childcare.

But single parents do not enjoy these same comforts. We are homebound with our children, unable to bring them on those necessary shopping trips out of fear for their safety and wellbeing. For a single parent, the time to shop is limited, and frequently, nonexistent. When those trips are possible, usually at the most inconvenient times, grocers' shelves may already be bare. For me, the

---

1 "The Majority of Children Live With Two Parents, Census Bureau Reports," United States Census Bureau, November 17, 2016, https://www.census.gov/newsroom/press-releases/2016/cb16-192.html.

fear of becoming infected with the virus during necessary outings lingers in the back of my mind—if I were to fall ill, who would watch my children? Who would provide their support? While I have been fortunate to have the ability to work from home and care for my daughters, I know of many other single parents who have not been quite as fortunate. I've also had the support of friends and family, who have offered to deliver groceries. Sadly, for many single parents, that lifeline does not exist. In this sense, I know I am better off than most.

These fears were realized in our home recently. My youngest daughter has a medical condition that places her at high risk if she were to become infected. In early April, she developed a fever. At once, my already precarious situation suddenly became one of life or death. My daughter's fever came on without warning. All efforts I had made to keep her safe seemed for naught. I watched as my older daughter, a survivor of trauma, entered a level of anxiety that threatened to shatter her already fragile mental state. The fears of the virus appeared to have become a reality despite my best efforts to prevent infection. We were already a statistic and now we were on the verge of upping the tally of the COVID-19 toll. Nervously, I phoned my pediatrician. I informed friends and family of the potential infection. There was nothing we could do except wait it out. While her fever broke within twenty-four hours, I spent the next week anxiously hoping that no other symptoms would appear. Serendipity visited us, and her condition improved. At the time this essay went to press, my daughters and I remained symptom free.

That is not to say that the fears were trivial. The isolation was already there. Our pediatrician was wonderful, but her hands were tied. Testing was, and remains, limited. Leaving home would have jeopardized the health of my daughters exponentially, with the risk of us all becoming infected if we were to seek medical treatment. In this time of crisis, those places that typically bring us peace of mind in an emergency—our physicians' offices and medical centers—are vectors of transmission. It was a primeval gut feeling knowing that we were indeed on our own. Our survival rested in our own hands. In reality, it rested in my hands alone. That is a dire set of consequences for any parent, and especially when parenting solo.

I knew I couldn't get sick. Two amazing lives were counting on me, as they always had, and now they needed me more than ever to remain strong. I am somewhat lucky in having a certain level of training in dealing with crisis situations from my brief military service that has served my daughters and I well through all of this. I am also a survivor, having overcome Lyme Disease and other personal setbacks. I have the will and means to go on living when others would crumble in the face of adversity. Still, I was tested. My resolve may not have wavered, but the fears and anxiety I felt were significant. Every moment I worried for my daughters' health and my own health—not out of concern for myself, but out of concern over their welfare, if I were to fall victim to the virus.

To some readers these circumstances may seem trivial. Some take the luxury of our medical system and first responders for granted. It is those members of society who place all of us at increased risk, and who are risking the lives of the members of the medical community fighting this pandemic under conditions suggestive of battlefield triage scenarios. Life and death have become a matter of who is fit for survival, who can be saved without straining the healthcare system, and likely, who will be able to benefit society once the curve has flattened. Seeing these behaviors suggests to me that priorities have not been adjusted to the new realities of living through a pandemic such as this one.

While we've all been made to readjust our lifestyles to a degree, it has certainly been easier for some than others. In certain ways, it is a mirror of how our society has always operated. But there is a much darker side to the plight of single-parent households in the U.S. Many single parents and their children are refugees. They have escaped violence and abuse. Life has already been a challenge, and now it is even more daunting. The fact remains that sheltering in place may have dire consequences for parents and their children struggling to flee a hostile home environment. With nowhere else to go, some remain in situations that pose imminent physical threats. If they have managed to escape, access to the court system for child support and other safety nets may have been delayed. While the criminal justice system remains intact, the fact is that single parents and their children continue to be at high risk from physical harm in these situations. The diminishment of economic and social safeguards only further jeopardizes these vulnerable members of society.

My daughters and I endured such a situation. We were fortunate to have ended it and to have become stable in our home before the quarantine measures were imposed. Had they been enacted sooner, that may not have been the case and our home life would not be the sanctuary it has become. For us, the timing was impeccable. Still, I am quick to remember that there are many who were not quite as lucky. These are the families forgotten amidst the pandemic. They continue to suffer in silence.

I remain hopeful that all is not grim. What the COVID-19 crisis has shown is that our society can change. Working from home for all families can be viable after this crisis has passed. Employers may come to recognize that productivity has not suffered and that employees are happier. Children spend more time at home. The financial burdens faced by all working families may ease somewhat. We may remain far from realizing this potential, but in the end, it is an ideal that is not out of reach. We are now living it under dire circumstances. Without the looming anxiety of a global pandemic, perhaps those with the power to enact change will do so and will make the ideal of the American family a truth and not an unobtainable fiction.

My daughters and I are seeing the benefits of this in our own lives. The rigors of juggling work, child-raising, and maintaining a home are not easy. However, as our situation has changed, the home has once again become a place of peace and healing. We remain a busy, modern family who have been given the benefit of slowing down. We enjoy the time alone. Days at the playground have been replaced with walks and bike rides. We cook meals together and enjoy them at the table as a family. We are a family again because we fled a dangerous situation, and because COVID-19 has given us the opportunity to be together without interruption. While the pandemic has caused concern, and I've noted that anxiety in my daughters, I am present to give them comfort and the age-appropriate knowledge to help relax their fears. Better yet, we have this time to heal from the pain of a not-so-distant past and restore our family. What the COVID-19 crisis has given us is the time to reflect on what matters most. It is, and always will be, the people we hold closest to us.

I've always held my daughters close. Unconditional love is that love between a parent and a child, and there is a trove of clichéd lines about this bond. However, they all fall short. We are all parents to the children of this world. To quote Toni Morrison, "When a kid walks in a room, your child or anybody else's child, does your face light up? That's what they're looking for." Wherever you are, be that light to the face of a child, especially now. In action, love is advanced. In love, there is hope.

Because, in the end, love always wins.

Harriet Levin Millan
Green Fox Fur

    (Recently I learned about Frieda Neiman's heroism upon reading an entry in the *Ozeryany Yiskor Book*. Ozeryany is the town in Western Ukraine where my grandmother's family lived before WWII. Numbering in the thousands and originally written in Yiddish, Yiskor books have only recently become available in English due to the efforts of a dedicated group of translators.)

Frieda Neiman refused to give
her green fox fur coat to the SS
who burst through her door. "*Better to die
in it than to let them have it*," she said.

Its ermine eyes keep watch, its throat,
a growl, she sets it around her shoulders,
as three heavy-booted SS, raise
their pistols, drag her between them,

so that only her toes touch ground,
and order her to *keep walking* over the thin spines
of leaves, their smell gone to musk
to a forest where other Jewish men and women

have been rounded up. Some of them stand above
a pit, the earth still sweet, and others inside it,
their corpses "stacked like wood,"
a squad leader later testified.

A solider aims and orders her to step
on a plank and strip. It's as if the springs on a trap fly
open. She leaps forward, knocks the pistol
out of the soldier's hands, fires back.

Another soldier swings his knife.
She grabs it, stabs him in his palm and runs
to the pine trees that crouch nearby,
waving to her with their arms open

when a pistol's deep hollow click enters her spine.
Then she falls. It snows all night.
Her brother Avram lies on top of the fresh
killed with this vision of his sister,

wrapped in her fur, running toward the pines,
in the moment before she is shot, coating his body,
torn at the seams, until dawn,
when he dares to take his first dazed steps.

                            • • •

Quilted, hooded, drawn in at the waist,
a fox fur hangs in my closet,

soft enough that I can stroke
the bellies and touch
the tapered hairs of the hundreds of animals
it took to make it.

Long ago, a boyfriend
bought it for me at the Goodwill to survive winters.

The immense racks filled with coats.
The screech of hangers.
The mirrors held us
as I twirled front to back
in fur after fur.

It was green, a color I had never seen
on a fur, green as sea waves
from a plane's window and wind
and bright green crickets.

Green gone to seed,
a fallow field
ready to be sown again.

If I met you, cousin,
would we share a resemblance?

My great grandmother,
Malka Majmann,
who stood rubbing the tip
of her boot in mud,

was the only one of seven siblings
to flee Ozeryany in time.

Ozeryany, a town known for its bookbinders,
glass blowers, cattle herders, poultry breeders,
weavers, tailors, tanners, a thriving market town,
on the limestone banks of the Dniester
where fish fossils trace back to the Pleistocene.

Each time I move
I reconsider
whether I should carry it along
Prodigal, it summons
the body's wildness,
the material revealed.
I lift it off its hanger
and bury
my face in it.

• • •

The black leather cover on the *Ozeryany Yiskor Book*
is embossed with an eternal lamp. Painted red,

it glows from a top shelf. With a librarian's help,
I am permitted to take down and hold,

etch with my finger and read the words
Frieda's brother Avram, conveyed to a handful
of *landschaften*, in that moment when he shook
off the snow that covered him to touch

the first spring sprigs that felt like hair
connecting him to what once was: the pastures, the bending
riverbank—that moment flows
through time to me. How else to describe

key pads installed on pre-school doors.
The anger of men who smashed a hundred gravestones

at Mt. Carmel, killed eleven congregants
at a synagogue baby naming. I thought
I wasn't being in the world anymore,
no being in the world or being of the world,

only hunted, so that space becomes a crosshair,
filled with the smell of smoke, no pretending to avoid it.

・・・

The library shelves shake,
the floor slopes,
the room is swirling,
ablaze in ultraviolet light.
The buttons on my blouse pop open,
my chest exposed.
My hands grow cold
to be given—*what?*—
the wind's crash?,
the creak of barn
doors back in Ukraine?
I hear a sound from far
away. It's horses' hooves.
They sound giddy,
thudding against the earth.
The horse hooves come
closer, carrying the scent
of smashed gooseberries.
I panic and fall forward.
My head hits
the library table,
but I don't feel any pain.
I'm numb all over,
like I'm about to give birth
and my perineum is stretched
so large it's tearing. She is in my body.

Gwen Ottinger
Make Your Writing Workshops Effective

The assignment was straightforward: Read a draft of a classmate's senior thesis and write a critique of it. As a brand-new college professor, I felt I was doing a good thing for my students. I explained to them that peer critiques would help them improve their theses—and their grades.

The peer critiques students turned in were not what I'd had in mind. "This is really good," some said, or "You're a great writer!" Others invoked writing dogma they learned in high school. "Don't use passive voice." "Your sentences are too long." I couldn't see how this feedback would help students improve their theses. I quietly abandoned the assignment.

I ran into the same problem again when I began taking creative writing workshops. I submitted my early attempts at short stories for critique and got feedback from my classmates that was evaluative ("This is terrific!") or prescriptive ("Your characters need more depth") but that didn't help me understand how to make my stories better.

I was tempted to abandon the workshops, just as I had the peer critique assignment. But deep down I knew I needed that feedback. I just couldn't put into words what I needed it for. Without understanding its purpose, I couldn't get what I needed from my creative writing workshops. I also couldn't explain to students how to give their peers the right kind of feedback. I saw the same confusion in the writers around me, and even in many workshop leaders. We all knew that feedback was good for us; we were less clear about why.

A decade of workshops, revisions, and peer critique experiments later, I can finally explain why we seek feedback on our writing. As authors, we want to know whether the words on the page are fulfilling our creative vision. Whether that vision has to do with making an argument or making a reader feel the pain of an unlikely hero, there is inevitably a gap between what we want our words to convey and how a reader experiences them. We hope that getting feedback from readers will help us close that gap.

Insightful critique can also help us clarify our creative vision. Few writers start out knowing exactly what we want to say and why. We discover it in the process of crafting the work. Hearing how readers understood the meaning of a piece can help us recognize our intentions. Readers may articulate a theme in a surprising new way. Or their misinterpretations may push us to blurt out what we *really* mean.

Ultimately, it is up to us as authors to measure readers' responses against our intentions. That's why feedback that is primarily evaluative or prescriptive—the kind of feedback I was seeing in my writing workshop and in students' peer critiques—is seldom helpful. A reader can't judge something "good" or advise the author on what she "should" do if he doesn't fully understand what the author is trying to achieve.

The best feedback is descriptive. It occurs when readers let the author know what the work is conveying to them. It occurs when readers share what they experienced as they read. With this kind of feedback, we authors can determine whether readers' experience is in line with what we meant to convey. If not, readers' observations can help point us to particular aspects of the text that aren't serving our vision in the way that we hoped.

Understanding how feedback should function for authors, I now approach peer critiques and workshops differently. As an instructor and as a reader, I look for ways to reflect back to authors what their work is accomplishing. I've found a number of strategies effective, and weave them into my peer critique assignments:

Summarize the work. Statements such as "The main point that I take away from this is…" or "For me, the major theme was…" can be invaluable in helping an author understand what is coming through, what isn't coming through, and where readers may be getting the wrong idea.

Share strong reactions. "I shuddered when the protagonist opened the door on p. 23," or "When you talked about the mother and the asthma meds, that's when I really got mad" can let an author know whether she is striking the right chords.

Give specific praise. "I loved the section about the garden, because I know exactly how that woman feels" is much more informative for an author than, "You're a great writer."

Identify points of confusion as specifically as possible. "On p. 16, I thought you meant one thing, but p. 45 seems like it says the opposite" or "I wasn't sure why that character would make that decision."

Ask questions about the author's vision. "How did you want us to feel about this?" and "What motivated you to write this piece?" can help an author articulate what he's trying to accomplish with his writing. Knowing more about an author's intentions can in turn help readers offer more useful comments and suggestions.

As an author, I also approach discussions of my work differently. When I submit a piece for workshopping, I know I want specific, descriptive feedback to help me close the gap between my draft and my intentions. So I ask readers questions tailored to elicit that kind of feedback. If someone says they like a character—or can't stand them—I'll try asking, "How would you describe that character?" or "What do you know about the character?" For an argumentative essay, I avoid asking, "Did you agree?" and instead ask "What piece of evidence did you find most powerful?" And when a reader expresses confusion, I try not to clarify right away, but wait for other readers to respond. Watching a group puzzle out a confusing aspect of my work can suggest both what I need to clarify and how best to do it.

Feedback is good for us. In fact, it's essential for authors to have the input of readers as they create and revise their work. But workshops and critiques are most effective when everyone involved understands that their purpose is to help authors understand and achieve their vision. The most powerful feedback reflects back to authors what they are accomplishing with their writing, so that they can move closer to what they *want* to accomplish.

Don Riggs
Review of Philip M. Cohen's *Nick Bones Underground*

Nick Bones Underground is a slipstream novel, combining elements of Science Fiction, Urban Fantasy, and the Crime/Detection genre. It is set in a vague time frame, given that at least one of the characters is a Holocaust survivor, albeit a very old one, and computer technology has advanced into the realm of Artificial Intelligence, which impacts the daily life of the narrator-protagonist, Nicholas Friedman, a professor of Comparative Religions at a university in New York City. Life in the city has been inflected by something which is referred to as the "Great Debacle," which is never completely explained or defined except at one point as having had to do with computers' developing a degree of free will and acting in unpredictable ways. The most evident example of this cybernetic behavior comes in the form of Maggie, the A.I. in the apartment of the narrator, who, having become a transgender computer, now yearns to become an incarnation of Marlene Dietrich.

Maggie has a very protective attitude towards the narrator, and acts in ways as a caretaker, heating up his breakfast coffee and hot cereal as well as doing online searches at his request. Prof. Friedman did a missing person search at a private individual's request, although he has no connection to the police department and up to that point had had no experience in locating the disappeared. However, he did find the individual, who at that point was just a skeleton, and this exploit earned him the moniker "Nick Bones" in the New York media.

Nick Bones Underground also has links to Yiddish culture; the plot setting from a story by the late Yiddish writer Chaim Grade, "My Quarrel with Hersh Rasseyner," where two boys who had grown up together studying in a yeshiva in Eastern Europe go separate ways, one becoming a secular Jew and the other an ultra-Orthodox rebbe. In *Nick Bones*, the narrator graduates from the yeshiva as a skeptic, possibly an agnostic, but retains his drive to consider the ultimate questions and concerns of religion in general, studying many faiths. His boyhood best friend, Shmulie Schimmer, an out-and-out nonbeliever, goes to a prestigious graduate school in chemistry, and makes a fortune by developing a designer drug that is both a psychedelic and a stimulant, but turns its users into unconscious vegetables in an apparently permanent coma. Shmulie's father, Abe, tracks down Nick Bones to locate his son, who has been missing for years.

   At this point, the search becomes a Descent Narrative, where Nick—despite the very emotional protests of Maggie, the A.I.—goes into the Velvet Underground, which is a subterranean city occupying an abandoned subway tunnel. What he encounters there is a fantasmagoric series of spaces occupied by a weird assortment of what may be called posthuman citizens who have escaped from aboveground New York City. As with many of the Descent Myths from the ancient world and their more modern counterparts, Nick encounters many elements from his own past that have led to his personal current state of affairs, as well as the residue of past societal trends and actions that have formed this near-post-apocalyptic reality. There are many allusions to 1960s pop culture, such as the Velvet Underground and Lou Reed, who is perhaps the model for Nick's walk on the wild side here.

One of the pleasures of reading this novel is that the author makes very understated mentions of things that, the reader comes to know, will emerge as significant foreshadowings of later events; these are so subtle, however, that it is easy to overlook them at the time. Some of this has to do with Nick's coming to awareness of his own culpability in the epidemic of the specific drug, which has taken many young people out of their lives full of promise to a permanent residence in a hospital bed, where they are comatose and simply turned over from time to time by nurses to prevent bedsores. There is an echo here of the opioid crisis in recent American society, as well as the practice of slipping roofies in other people's drinks.

The occurrence of Yiddish words adds to the overall flavor of the novel's setting, which is good, although it is possible that for readers who do not "speak Jewish," as my Russian-born grandma put it, they will have difficulty knowing whatever they mean. For science fiction readers, who simply take for granted that not all of the technical terms will be "real," this would be no problem, and the same for people who can get the basic idea of what a *"nudnik"* is or *"mishigas,"* although the author follows the mention of *"davenning"* at one point with a description of what the people davenning are doing, that serves almost as a definition. Perhaps people should read *Nick Bones Underground* with a copy of Leo Rosten's *The Joys of Yiddish* handy; there could also be, in the book's next edition, a brief Glossary for the Goyim.

Ultimately, this novel is a Mad Scientist narrative. It is as if Dr. Jekyll had, after developing his miracle elixir, released it to the world under the canny ministrations of a highly efficient marketer. *Nick Bones Underground* in addition explores the complex web of interconnectedness and shared responsibility in the context of a tapestry of sects of a religion inflected by Artificial Intelligence and Virtual, if not virtuous, Reality. Despite the fact that this is really a very funny novel, there are some very significant ethical issues raised here, and while some of the morals of the story are fairly obvious, there are also some issues that are not so easily resolved.

Errol Craig Sull
"Didja"—Word of the Year from COVID

COVID has changed many highways, avenues, paths, and byways of our lives. And although the vaccine gives us that much sought-after and prayed for "light at the end of the tunnel" many of these changes will be longer term, if not permanent. For example, online shopping for groceries has exploded, and so many folks have discovered this as a new way to "go to market" that its uptick is undoubtedly a permanent one. And spending so much time at home has birthed new bakers, home repair specialists, and TV junkies—might these also remain? But what about our language: no doubt a new word has entered into millions of households, a new word that will probably dissipate, if not disappear, once the pandemic ends. But while here it sure is one fun yet nettlesome word: "didja."

I found myself discovering this word in the first few weeks of home isolation, muttering to my wife, Cathy: "Didja ever notice how long that flower stays open on our African Violet?" … "Didja know I have 14 books on grammar in my bookcase?" … "Didja ever notice how long it took for the buds on our trees to open?" … "Didja know there were two stations with reruns of *Gunsmoke*?" She thought me a crazy man, but I couldn't help myself: "Didja," it seems, became my mantra of in-home isolation.

Once summer rolled around my "Didjas" seemed to really bloom: "Didja ever notice how many folks on our street walk their dogs?" … "Didja know our morning paper is delivered at 5:30 am almost every day?" … "Didja ever count the number of branches on our big maple? There are 77!" … "Didja know our dishwasher took 55 minutes from start to finish?" … "Didja ever notice we have three different shades of wood on our living room floor?"

Of course, the fall and early winter brought many more wonderful "Didjas" into my life, and I could not deny any. I asked Cathy, "Didja happen to notice how many squirrel nests we have in our trees?" … "Didja know we have four cans of pureed pumpkin and 5 tubes of almond paste in the basement?" … "Didja ever notice how many foods of unknown origin we have in the back of our freezer?" … "Didja know we have four snow shovels, six trowels, and three hammers in our garage?" … "Didja ever notice how much more time we spend on Facebook and Instagram?"

I can assure you: I was a normal person before "Didja " entered my life—work, family, exercise, hobbies. And while these are still the majority of my life it seems that every day brings another "Didja." Oh, my wife tolerates me; she thinks of my "Didjas" as harmless mutterings of a man who longs for life before COVID. Its isolation has brought "Didjas" to many people, muttering day in and day out, "Didja ever notice …" and "Didja know …" And the "Didja" possibilities are seemingly endless: every nook of a house, every cranny of the outdoors, every slip of a grocery store.

The pandemic is an ugly, horrific, deadly event in our lives; it cannot end too soon so the number of hospitalizations and deaths can fade, then eventually disappear. And, yes, with this ending will hopefully come the quiet and gratefully appreciated rest of my "Didjas." If not I'm fearful of the so many unexplored "Didjas" waiting for me, beckoning me. By the way, didja notice how many words are in this piece? And didja notice how many periods and didja see …

Scott Warnock
Let's Watch the News Together

We're all aware of some version of *the problem*: It's not just that we can't agree, it's that we can't even have the conversation.

You know what I'm talking about. In a way, it's difficult to articulate—challenging to find the right words to explain. You say something and I'm immediately sent spinning. I say something and you have a fact to refute it.

You're suspicious. So am I. We've both heard things and have data and sources. We both have premises. We both know a lot of stuff. Over and over, we keep having conversations that never get off the ground.

Even though *we're* still connected, we know those who've separated from friends and family.

So let's try something different, something kind of simple—if we'll give it a chance.

Let's watch the news together.

Yes, this is an invitation. In these COVID times, we don't have to be in the same room. Let's get on the old horn, settle down, and watch the news. Let's flip the channels and land on one. You tell me what you see. I'll tell you what I see. You tell me what you hear. I'll tell you what I hear.

Then we'll flip to another channel. You can pick the first channel. I'll pick the second. Repeat.

Let's present our experience to each other so we start to understand not so much what each other thinks—which all of us may be too eager to volunteer lately—but try to understand how each other *sees the world*.

I need to understand that if I'm asking this of you, I have to hold up my end. I can't immediately swoop in if I hear something I don't like. I can't sit, ready to pounce on the perceived weakness (when you think about it, it's amazing how many of the metaphors for these types of behaviors draw from images of hunting or attacking animals) of your argument.

Basically, I have to shut my mouth for a minute and hear what you have to say, but *over the specific medium of watching the news together*. So we're freeing each other of squabbling about vague data points and generalized conspiracies. We're watching images on the screen and listening to the words that accompany them, and we say, "I see this. I hear this."

We have come a long way on the trail of life, but we know we probably won't end up agreeing. I don't want us to bicker, but we may start arguing a bit. Perhaps that's okay, but let's just not finish that way.

Because if we can't even do this simple thing, take a few minutes and watch TV together, then all hope for discourse really is lost, isn't it?

Part of me envisions a scenario in which we don't even weigh in on each other's comments. We listen, take our turn, and eventually turn the TV off and take conversation elsewhere, maybe to why we've been friends all the years, or why we became friends in the first place.

Then we can hang up for now.

Contributors

Jordan Anderson is a Communications major with a concentration in journalism. At the moment, she is in the midst of receiving the Certificate in Writing and Publishing. She chose communications as her major because she is passionate about the crucial role the media plays in our society. Specifically, she is interested in broadcast communications. She is also passionate about civic engagement and making the world a better place for disadvantaged communities. In her free time, she enjoys crocheting and making new creations.

Jan Armon was born at the midpoint of the twentieth century, and stubbornly clings to life by absorbing, even over Zoom, the life force of his students—while each day a few of them awake to find scattered grey hairs. He acquired this level of moral turpitude through his initial profession, the law. Yet by 1981, Jan had tired of earning an actual living and so decided to pursue a Ph.D. in English at the University of Michigan. There he discovered a liking for the course other doctoral candidates taught only grudgingly, freshman composition. To keep things light, however, Jan teaches courses on the murder mystery, too.

Vivek Babu is a first-year student at Drexel University, where he majors in Biology through the BS/MD program. He plans to pursue medical school in the future and ultimately hopes to promote equitable healthcare systems with a special focus on immigrant health. Vivek is currently a staff writer at the *National Collegiate Journal of Science* (NCJS), where he leads "HIPPOCRATES," which strives to dissect disparities in medicine, and "History of Discovery," which looks at the history of modern scientific achievement. Outside of writing, Vivek serves as the freshman class vice president of the Undergraduate Student Government Association and a member of Beta Beta Beta. In his free time, Vivek enjoys overanalyzing movies, making Spotify playlists, and exploring the city.

Emma Barnes is a Biomedical Engineering major. She wanted to emphasize the pitfalls of the fashion industry in her argumentative essay. As an individual (and amateur seamstress) that has always been fascinated by fashion and clothing production, she sought to bring attention to a global issue many consumers will never truly understand. Emma looks to continue writing expository pieces during her five-year pursuit of a concentration in Biomechanics and Human Performance Engineering at Drexel. She also hopes readers will use this information to change their buying habits and spread the word in favor of a brighter future.

Kelly Bergh is a graduate of the Drexel University Masters in Publishing program. She has helped to design and create numerous Writers Room publications, including *Quaranzine 2020: A New Ritual*.

Mikayla Butz-Weidner is a third year English major, a student in the Pennoni Honors College, and Editor-in-Chief of *The Triangle*. She enjoys the works of T.S. Eliot, all things Connecticut, and The Beach Boys. She comes from the greater Philadelphia area but will likely end up in London. Her writing has largely remained private, and this is her first time publishing work in several years.

Nicky Como is a Biology major pursuing the pre-med track. She enjoys writing, drawing, and painting in her free time. Nicky writes for Drexel's independent student run newspaper, *The Triangle*. She wrote for her high school newspaper as well and fell in love with op-ed writing ever since.

Ellie DiPaolo is a first-year Fashion Design student at Drexel University from Houston, Texas. Her love of reading began at a young age and progressed into writing throughout her time in the journalism department of her middle and high school. She is thrilled to publish her first piece at Drexel. In her free time, Ellie enjoys baking, fashion, and exploring Philadelphia.

Eden Skye Einhorn ('21) is a writer and visual artist. For her senior project (Fashion Design), she created her own fabric.

Valerie Fox has published prose in *Juked, Cleaver, Reflex, NFFR, Okay Donkey, Across the Margin*, and other journals. Her books include *The Rorschach Factory* and *Insomniatic*. She's had stories selected for the "Best Small Fictions" and "Best Microfictions" series. Much interested in collaboration, she published *The Real Sky* (art/word collaboration), a limited edition, hand-made book, with artist Jacklynn Niemiec.

Ana Fuciu is a first-year international student at Drexel University, majoring in Film & Television. Areas of interest include film and documentary production, but she also loves writing creative non-fiction. For her, an ideal career would combine all of the interests mentioned above along with travelling around the world. She wants to help people with stories told through video and writing.

Max Gallagher (they/them) is a queer, nonbinary interdisciplinary artist. They are currently studying Mathematics and Dramatic Writing, and in the future, they hope to help their fellow humans to find peace. To experience more of Max's work (including essays, plays, and original songs) feel free to explore their cute little blog at maxvingal.wordpress.com.

Caroline Gallen is an undergraduate Biology student at Drexel University who hopes to become a researcher in the future. She doesn't quite know what she'll be researching, but she hopes it will be something that will help better the world. In the meantime, Caroline will continue going to school, reading and writing short stories on the side, volunteering, and blasting loud, irreverent rock music.

María José Garcia is a second-year student from Honduras pursuing a Bachelor of Science in Biomedical Engineering. She is passionate about bridging the gap between scientific research and its implementation in low-income areas and in developing countries. María José is also the Student Life Committee Chair of the Undergraduate Student Government Association (USGA) where she has focused her work on improving resources for students' mental health, supporting victims of sexual harassment and discrimination, and fostering a safe environment for all students regardless of their background. With her involvement in her community and in several organizations around campus, she hopes to one day inspire little girls around the world to pursue their dreams. Besides her advocacy work, she enjoys learning new things, reading, and dancing.

Sophie Geagan is a third-year Biology major and Chemistry minor. Her poetry was previously published in *The 33rd* in 2019 and she has been an active writer for Drexel's *Maya* literary magazine throughout her time at Drexel. Outside of poetry, her literary interests include reading Shakespeare plays with the Pennoni Honors College and mystery novels in her free time. After she graduates, Sophie hopes to attend medical school and become a physician.

Tim Hanlon is a Biology major (class of '21) in the College of Arts and Sciences and has won the humor category of the DPG Writing contest for the past 3 years. Tim also served as the Student Body President his senior year and over his 4-year Drexel tenure created the University's first Office of Sustainability. Upon graduating, Tim will be continuing his research on prostate and bladder cancer treatment at Harvard Medical School and the Dana Farber Cancer Institute. Outside of academics, Tim is a volunteer tutor at *SquashSmart*, an avid runner, and an ice cream connoisseur.

Muntaha Haq is a freshman studying General Business in the LeBow College of Business. Her most recent publications have been under the Arts & Entertainment section in Drexel University's newspaper, *The Triangle*. Muntaha has also been involved in the TEDx LeBow event, where she presented a speech on name discrimination earlier this fall. Muntaha's interests include theater, writing, and community outreach.

Sky Harper is a Navajo student from Arizona. He grew up surrounded by cultural teachings and his family. He enjoys incorporating his values and culture into his writing. He is an undergraduate Chemistry major who loves to read, write, cook, and laugh.

Jordan Hyatt is an Associate Professor in the Department of Criminology and Justice Studies, and Director for the Center for Public Policy.

Henry Israeli is the author of four collections of poetry, most recently *Our Age of Anxiety*, winner of the White Pine Press Poetry Prize.

Dejah Jade is a photographer and aspiring fashion designer. She's a graduate of Robeson High School ('19). She always makes clothes that she would wear and hopes to attend Drexel University, and to continue making new clothes that reflect her personality. For Writers Room in the spring of 2021, she co-curated and photographed an exhibition of portraits of Robeson High School seniors.

Kirsten Kaschock is a 2019 Pew Fellow in the Arts and Summer Literary Seminars grand prize winner and the author of five poetry books. The most recent, *Explain This Corpse*, won the Blue Lynx Prize from Lynx House Press. Coffee House Press published her debut speculative novel—*Sleight*.

Miriam N. Kotzin teaches creative writing and literature at Drexel University. Her short fiction, *Country Music* (Spuyten Duyvil Press 2017), joins a novel, *The Real Deal* (Brick House Press 2012), and a collection of flash fiction. She is the author of five collections of poetry, most recently, *Debris Field* (David Robert Books 2017). Her micros have been published in or are forthcoming in *Blink Ink*, *50-Word Stories*, *Doorknobs & Body Paint*, and *Five Minutes*.

Dylan Lam is a Junior Film and Television major at Drexel. He's an editor, cinematographer, photographer, and writer. Currently, he serves as Content Director at Apex Gaming PCs, a gaming PC company based in Philadelphia.

More of Dylan's photos, videos, and stories can be found at iamdylanlam.com. He's thrilled to have a photograph of his grace the cover of *The 33rd* for the second time!

Lynn Levin is a poet, writer, translator, and member of Drexel's Department of English and Philosophy. Her essays, fiction, and poetry have been published in *The Massachusetts Review* blog, *Hawaii Pacific Review*, *Michigan Quarterly Review*, *The Smart Set*, *Boulevard*, *The Saturday Evening Post*, and many other places. She is the author of five collections of poems, most recently *The Minor Virtues* (Ragged Sky, 2020). Her website is lynnlevinpoet.com.

George A. MacMillan is an Adjunct Professor of Writing at Drexel University. Writing under the pen name H.A. Callum, his debut novel, *Whispers in the Alders*, was published by Brown Posey Press in 2018. His poetry, short fiction, and essays have appeared in several online and print journals. Mr. MacMillan received his B.A. in English from the Pennsylvania State University (summa cum laude) and is enrolled in Drexel University's MFA Creative Writing program.

Alina Macneal teaches architecture classes at Drexel University in the Antoinette Westphal College of Media Arts & Design, as well as with the Pennoni Honors College. She's a poet and longtime member of the Writers Room workshop.

Harriet Levin Millan is the author of three poetry books and a novel. Her books have received prizes from the Poetry Society of America, Independent Publishers, the Ellen La Forge Memorial Poetry Foundation, and Barnard New Women Poets. She was the founding director of Drexel's University Writing Program, and she presently teaches writing in the English Department and MFA program at Drexel and directs the Certificate Program in Writing and Publishing. She is faculty advisor to The Drexel PEN Society, the first undergraduate PEN America chapter in North America. "Green Fox Fur" was selected by Natalie Diaz as a finalist for *Hunger Mountain*'s 2019 Ruth Stone Poetry Prize. It was published in *Hamilton Stone Review*, Spring 2021.

Gwen Ottinger is an Associate Professor at Drexel University, in the Department of Politics and the Center for Science, Technology, and Society. She directs the Fair Tech Collective, a research group that uses social science theory and methods to promote social justice in science and technology. She has received a CAREER award from the U.S. National Science Foundation for her research on "Environmental Justice and the Ethics of Science and Technology" and the 2015 Rachel Carson Prize from the Society for Social Studies of Science for her book, *Refining Expertise: How Responsible Engineers Subvert Environmental Justice Challenges*. Ottinger is a 2020 ACLS-Burkhardt Fellow and was a 2020-2021 Fellow at the Center for Advanced Study in the Behavioral Sciences (CASBS) at Stanford University.

Elsa Panczner is an Animation & Visual Effects student in the Westphal College of Media Arts & Design. After graduating, she intends to work in film and produce small independent projects on the side. Outside of school, Elsa has a passion for weightlifting and encourages others to join her healthy lifestyle. In her art and her writing, Elsa aspires to portray the authentic world.

Anh Quach is a pre-junior studying Biological Sciences with a minor in Food Science. She is from Vietnam and aspires to become a microbiologist, so that she can work full-time with bacteria. When she is not studying, running experiments in the lab, or sleeping, she enjoys experimenting with her hair color, playing the piano, singing, and going for walks. Her writings are inspired by her upbringing in urban Vietnam, and her most recent work was published in the 2019 edition of *The 33rd*.

Sanjana Ramanathan is an undergraduate English major at Drexel University with a concentration in Writing. She enjoys writing poetry, essays, and fictional short stories. Her hobbies include reading and playing video games. Her essay previously published by *The 33rd*, "An End to Sexism in Gaming Communities," has been included in the newest edition of W.W. Norton's textbook *They Say / I Say*.

Don Riggs (he/him/his) has been reading science fiction since 5th grade (1962-63) and has been writing reviews of science fiction and fantasy works since 1985 because it is a good way to get free books that have just been published and to practice his analytical writing skills. Since then, he has earned a B.A. majoring in Myth, an M.A. and Ph.D. in Comparative Medieval Literature, and an M.A. in Creative Writing.

Aaliyah Sesay is a 2020 Drexel graduate with a B.A. in English. She currently works with nonprofits, serving Philadelphia's youth, and continues to work on her short fiction pieces.

Arthi Sivendra is a first-year Philosophy, Politics, and Economics student at Drexel University. She likes to spend her time painting, crocheting, and reading. While she does not have much writing experience outside of the classroom, she does greatly enjoy the process.

Errol Craig Sull is an Adjunct Instructor in the English Department Drexel University. He has taught at Drexel for twelve years. His recognitions include "Dell Online Educator of Excellence." He writes two national columns on distance learning, has five published books, and various published essays (including such diverse publications as *The Atlantic* and *American Horticulturalist*). Previously, Errol was Cultural Editor at *Southern Living* magazine and Assistant Editor at *The National Enquirer*.

Kala F. Summers is a Global Studies major with a concentration of Global Health & Sustainability. Summers currently minors in Asian Studies and hopes to minor in Public Health and Photography in the future. Summers has a strong passion for film and digital photography as well as research. Currently, she runs a popular food blog on Instagram called @uhungrysis, that aims to generate exposure for local businesses that have been affected by the COVID-19 pandemic, while also showcasing food businesses for local college students. In just a few short months, @uhungrysis has gained a large following and partnered with restaurants in Philadelphia. Summers is proud of the opportunities she has experienced at Drexel University and hopes to continue to grow during her remaining years

Sanjana Suresh is a freshman at the LeBow College of Business within Drexel

University, currently majoring in Operations & Supply Chain Management and Business Analytics. She is actively involved in a variety of organizations on campus, including Drexel's Undergraduate Student Government Association, Drexel Women in Business, and Drexel Dandiya. She also serves as an Undergraduate Research Assistant to Dr. Thomas Heverin and recently co-wrote a 10-page conference paper on the use of semantic-web technologies in automating situation assessment tasks performed by ethical hackers. In her free time, Sanjana enjoys spending time with her friends and family, reading, writing, and playing lacrosse.

Abby Tabas is currently a first-year Exploratory Studies major who is considering pursuing computer science and/or product design at Drexel. She enjoys baking and creating art in her spare time.

Marie Ann Tomaj is Biology major at Drexel University. She enjoys reading and writing in her free time as well as learning about things happening in the world. She would like to use her interest in research and writing to bring into light events and topics that are often forgotten despite their importance.

Lianna Wang is a first-year Interactive Digital Media student at the Antoinette Westphal College of Media Arts and Design. She is passionate about creating things, whether the final product is a written work, design, or painting. In her free time, Lianna enjoys drawing, embroidering, and playing instruments.

Scott Warnock is a professor of English and Director of the University Writing Program at Drexel. He teachers a variety of courses and is widely published in the areas of online writing instruction, computers and composition, and education technology. Warnock is immediate past president of the Global Society of Online Writing Educators. He is president of the Palmyra High School Foundation for Educational Excellence and has coached youth sports in his local area since 2005. He writes the bi-weekly blog/column "Virtual Children" for the Website *When Falls the Coliseum*.

Sam Weinstein is an Environmental Studies and Sustainability major with a strong interest in sociology. Some of his hobbies include fashion, drawing, photography, painting, reading poetry and philosophy, and listening to lots of music. This is his first published work of writing.

Gabby Werner is an English major from New York. She enjoys reading horror novels, fishing, and playing video games. Her piece, "*Frankenstein*, Scientific Advancement, and the God Complex," was written for a class on romanticism and inspired by a desire to study the god complex in a different light.

Bethany White grew up in Baltimore, Maryland for the majority of her life before moving to Roanoke, Virginia the summer before her freshman year in college. She has been an avid reader her entire life and has a passion for telling stories. Bethany is currently a Freshman studying Architecture and she hopes to help the world and contribute to society with her future career.

Cianni Williams is a Secondary Education major with a focus on Social Studies at Drexel University. Born and raised in Philadelphia, she has found her passions in both creative writing and civic engagement, and when combined, she was able to create a collection of short stories centered around women of color. In her free time, Cianni enjoys watching thoughtful films, discovering new books, and spending quality time with her cats.

Hope Wilson is a Mechanical Engineering major and loves working with robotics. Outside of essays for classes, she dabbles in poetry and short stories. She spends her free time making music, collecting playing cards, and binge-watching seasons of whatever show captures her interest.

Want to appear in the 2022 edition of *The 33rd*?

All Drexel students and faculty are eligible

For more information visit
drexelpublishing.com